THE ASHFORD BOOK OF
D Y E I N G

ANN MILNER STUDIED ART, ceramics and weaving at Coventry Teacher Training College in England. Her weaving tutor was the late Constance Towers.

In 1967 she emigrated to New Zealand and began a study of New Zealand flora for her book on natural dyeing, *Natural Wool Dyes and Recipes*, which was published in 1971.

For three years she was natural dye adviser to 'The Web' magazine published by the New Zealand Spinning, Weaving and Woolcrafts Society. During this period of time she returned to weaving and was invited to exhibit in the Merke Sharpe and Dohme 'Golden Fleece' exhibition.

Study projects on fibres and methods of spinning, which were produced for her tutoring purposes, became the basis for *I Can Spin a Different Thread*, published in 1979.

Ann Milner specializes in handwoven fabrics, using handspun yarns which are dyed and blended from fibre to finished fabrics, designed for clients and galleries. Her current interest is in wall fabrics, which are to look at rather than to wear, and often contain areas of dyed cotton woven into the background.

Ann Milner tutors for the New Zealand Spinning, Weaving and Woolcraft Society, for WEA, and for the Otago Polytechnic.

THE ASHFORD BOOK OF
DYEING

Ann Milner

First published in New Zealand in 1992 by
Bridget Williams Books Limited, P.O. Box 9839, Wellington, New Zealand

ISBN 0 908912 25 0

A Shoal Bay Press book
Printed in Hong Kong through
Bookprint Consultants Ltd, Wellington

CONTENTS

ACKNOWLEDGMENTS

With gratitude, I would like to acknowledge many people who have helped me
through my paths of learning and experimentation.

Maxine Lovegrove introduced me to percentage dyeing, enabling me to reproduce
a dye shade. Kelly Thompson and Helen Budd shared their knowledge of dyes for
cellulose fibres, so that I could venture into new areas of creativity. Sally McLean's
enthusiasm for dyeing in a microwave oven encouraged me to use this rapid heat
source, which has proved invaluable, especially for sampling dyes. Thanks also to:
Maewyn Wells, whose feltmaking I have enjoyed, but not yet tried for myself;
Daniella Sperber, who sent her recipe for fixing Procion dyes with sodium silicate;
Molly Duncan, who sent many books from her collection to aid my research; and
Rosemarie Jones, who kindly appraised the script on naphthol dyes. When I was
researching natural dye materials, I received considerable help from Fred Gerber of
Florida, from Janet McKenzie and Annie Clarke from New Zealand.

The photograph on p. 109 is by the artist, Kelly Thompson. All other photography
by Lindsay McLeod FPS, Dunedin, New Zealand. I should like to express my great
appreciation for the quality of Lindsay's work and the tremendous help he offered to
Richard Ashford and me during the preparation of this book.

Thanks to Carolyn Landis for the loan of the Japanese purses and the kimono on
pp. 123 and 124, and to the Otago Museum for the batik textile on p. 122.

I wish to thank chemical companies and dye distributors who answered my
queries without hesitation.

I should like to thank Richard Ashford of Ashford Handicrafts for giving me the
opportunity to write this book.

Ann Milner

INTRODUCTION

The stages of my creative development have been like a series of doors opening before me, giving me access to new knowledge of fibres, craft techniques or dyes and colour. The intention of this book is to open doors for you.

I have begun with natural dyeing. This is where I started in the late 1950s when chemical dyes were less successful than today, and not readily available in small quantities. There is a feeling of harmony with the natural environment that comes with collecting natural dyestuffs, bringing them into the home and extracting their dyes to transfer onto yarns and fibres, especially if the yarns are handspun. Yarns dyed from vegetable origins have an underlying golden warmth which, like a common bond, enables all natural shades to blend together in immediate harmony. However, we must play our part by being aware of natural resources, so that we do not in any way deplete nature.

When I lived in Great Britain I used many plants that are not available in New Zealand, but the dyes in this book are from dyestuffs that surround me now. The joy of natural dyeing is in the seeking, testing and finding a new or unknown dye. It is an obsession, so please be warned!

Not all of nature's colours are fast to light, especially here in New Zealand. To create an item which subsequently fades or partially fades, is so disappointing, especially if it is a gift, an exhibition entry, or a saleable product, and for this reason all of the dyes have been ruthlessly tested and documented.

I found it exciting to be part of the huge revival of interest in spinning and weaving in the mid-1960s, but at first everything was produced in the natural shades of white, grey and black. I remember thinking that the pottery glazes were the same colours. The standard of technical skills and expertise soon became evident, but colour was much slower to erupt.

Natural dyeing became an obvious complement to handspun yarns, but there was always the problem of availability of dyestuff in sufficient quantities at the required time. Consequently when acid dyes for natural fibres became available in small amounts they were eagerly sought by hobbyist and craftperson alike. Initially they were used with little skill. Hasty dyeing produced patchy results, and a reluctance to blend the dyes together made some colours instantly recognisable. It was obvious that some method for mixing dyes in a manner that could be repeated was needed, and percentage dye classes were very popular. This stage was crucial to me as a producer of handwoven fabrics for clients requiring certain shadings for their wardrobes. Percentage dyeing allowed me to experiment until I arrived at exactly the colour ordered. I became surrounded by hundreds of tiny hanks of yarn in a multitude of colours. Newer fibre reactive dyes also came onto the market, and so my collection of dyed yarns increased, and continues to grow.

My reason for interest in dyeing cellulose fibres was twofold. Cotton yarns had been used far more in Britain than in New Zealand and I was already aware of the clarity of colour when they are dyed. Secondly I felt that handpainted silk scarves should complement my handwoven tweeds, and the cotton dyes are also suitable for silk. Since acquiring some knowledge of these fibre reactive dyes I have used dyed cotton in my weaving and explored batik, shibori and kasuri. This book is not intended to be a work manual on these subjects, but I have included a few ideas to encourage the beginner.

Colour is not easy to talk about because we all respond to it in different ways at different times and emotional responses lead to personal colour choices. We are influenced by fashion changes, our personal colouring, by the great master painters, or by our environmental surroundings. Some basic understanding of colour will however help to make sound selections. For instance, complementary colours can be placed beside each other in the correct proportions, when viewed as flat areas of colour such as wall hangings; but when twisted together during the spinning or weaving process, they produce dull muddy shades when viewed from a distance. I have met many people who were afraid of colour because they did not know where to start, and to a certain extent I believe that this led to a reluctance to use chemical dyes. I therefore hope that the section on colour will give courage to those people. It is far better to understand why certain colours relate to each other, than to merely copy groups of colour harmonies prepared by specialists.

Successful dyeing is based upon a sound bond between dye and fibre. Each dye has certain requirements and each class of dyestuff will be more suited to one fibre than another. You need a little knowledge and understanding of dye procedure to become a confident dyer. This book includes recipes I needed, answers to questions I have asked, and the results from my personal research, trials and errors – all simply explained yet thorough in approach for the would-be, and experienced dyer.

There is a kaleidoscope ready for us to use, and another door is ready to open.

Ann Milner

1. GETTING STARTED

INTRODUCTION

Before setting out on the exciting world of creating colour on fibres and fabric, take a moment to study the table of contents on pp 5–6. Chapter Two deals solely with natural dyeing – an area with great potential for experimentation and surprises. There are many modern, easy to use chemical dyes giving a wonderful range of colours. These, together with many of the older dyes and dye types, are discussed in Chapters Three to Nine.

The effect you wish to achieve, the dye and the dyeing procedure you choose and the type of fabric or fibre you wish to dye are all interrelated. Your first task is to identify your fibre (see below).

You will see that the chapters on chemical dyeing are organized according to fibre type and dyeing procedure. Early in each of these chapters is a summary of dyes suitable for your fabric, giving dye classes and brand names. If you are unable to trace a specific dye, try to establish the dye class to which it belongs and follow the relevant instructions.

FIBRES AND FABRICS

Animal fibres

Animal fibres, including human hair, may be referred to as protein fibres since they are composed of protein in the form of amino acids. These acids vary in type and number from one animal fibre to another and consequently wool, for instance, may give a slightly different shade from alpaca when dyed. However animal fibres will all react to the dye in a similar way. Included in the list will be wool, angora, alpaca, mohair, cashmere, cashgora, camel and dog hair.

Animal fibres resist a flame when a burning test is applied, burning only whilst held in the flame. A soft black ash is formed and the smell of burning hair or feathers is given off.

Silk

Silk is also a protein fibre, even though it has been secreted rather than grown, and dyes suitable for wool will also be suitable for silk, providing that the safe upper temperature limit of 84°C or 185°F, is observed. Beyond this limit it is damaged. Dyes designed for cellulose fibres will also dye silk.

Nylon

Nylon is a synthetic fibre. It reacts with dyes in an acidic situation and dyes to darker value and to a greater intensity than animal fibres. Any dye which is suitable for protein fibre will also dye nylon, but you will need to use less dye to achieve the same shade. Nylon does not need Glauber's salt to retard the dye, because it can be stirred regularly to aid levelling without felting occurring.

Cellulose fibres

Cellulose or vegetable fibres are all produced by plants, and have a chemical structure similar to sugars and starches. Bast fibres come from the stringy inner stalks of the plants. Others are made from leaves or seed pods.

Jute
A low grade harsh fibre which yellows when exposed to light. It is used mainly for utility goods such as sacks.

Hemp
A stronger and softer fibre than jute, produced from an Indian herbaceous plant.

Ramie
Sometimes called china grass or rhea, Ramie is produced from a nettle plant. It is naturally white, very lustrous and resembles soft linen.

Flax
Linen is sometimes referred to as flax; other flax plants produce a poorer fibre than linen. For example New Zealand flax, *Phormium tenax*, produces a brown coarse fibre, not as strong as linen.

Linen
The finest linen is produced from the fibre of the plant *Linum usitatissimum.*

Sisal
A strong fibre prepared from the leaves of the agave plant.

Cotton
Produced from the fine fibres surrounding the seeds of the cotton plant.

Manufactured cellulose

Rayon
A man-made fibre with a cellulose structure, and is dyed with the same dyes used for vegetable fibres.

PREPARATION OF FIBRES AND FABRICS FOR DYEING

Lanolin and dirt in fleeces, spinning oil and sizing on yarns, and starches and bleaches on fabrics, all prevent the dyes, mordants and additives from penetrating the fibres. The areas reached first by the dyes will be a darker shade; an oily spot will receive less dye and the result will be streaky uneven dyeing. In the same manner dye will penetrate wet areas before dry areas, and for this reason we always thoroughly wet all yarns, fibres and fabrics for at least 20 minutes before squeezing out the excess liquid and entering them into dye or mordant, to ensure even dyeing. Special finishes in fabrics such as permanent press, cannot be removed, so do not dye these fabrics.

Weigh the yarns or fibre before scouring so that you can work out how much dye to use. If the fibre is really dirty and greasy, you may need to wash it and dry it again before weighing it, in order to get an accurate reading.

Animal fibres

Silk, wool, mohair, cashmere, alpaca and camel, can all be scoured by soaking them in warm water (50°C, 120°F) to which a neutral detergent has been added. This is my preference because it is easy to wash out of the fibre and being neither acid nor alkaline, it does not affect subsequent dyes. Avoid temperature shocks between soaking, dyeing or rinsing stages, or the fibres become damaged. Handle the fibres gently at each stage to avoid felting.

Wool

Before washing a fleece I weigh it. I usually estimate that 20% of the weight of a moderately clean crossbred fleece will be grease. A fine merino or halfbred could contain as much as 50% weight of grease. To make absolutely sure, however, it is better to wash and fully dry the fleece to get an accurate weight.

I treat all fleece types in the same way. Wet fleece is very heavy to handle, so I usually wash half a fleece at a time. I use my laundry tub, because I can remove the plug and allow the water to drain away by itself without removing the fleece until after the final rinse. You can wash smaller amounts in a bucket or kitchen sink if you prefer, but allow room for the fleece to expand when wet.

Using either a large sink or a large container, I part fill it with hot water to which liquid detergent has been added. I use three buckets of water (30 litres) at a temperature between 50–60°C (120–140°F) and 20 ml (2 dessertspoons) of detergent.

Drop the fleece into the warm detergent water and push it gently below the surface of the water. Do not move it any more than this; merely allow it to absorb the warm water. Leave it to cool, then remove the plug and let the water drain away. You can push the fleece against one side to remove any excess. Replace the plug and pour over another three buckets (30 litres) of warm water, this time using 10ml (1 dsp) of detergent, and repeat the soaking and draining when the water is cool. Two rinses in clear warm water in the same fashion should leave the fleece quite clean and free from grease. It is now ready to mordant and dye.

Should you not require the fleece immediately and would prefer it dry, squeeze out any excess water and place the fleece in a muslin bag or a pillow slip. Spin it for one minute in a washing machine on spin cycle, then leave it in a warm shady place to dry. **Never** put animal fibres into a tumbler dryer or heated dryer because they will felt quite rapidly.

Angora

Since rabbits secrete very little lanolin angora needs very little scouring, but it does need a longer wetting out time of 30–40 minutes. Alkalis damage this delicate fibre. If angora is to be dyed in the fibre rather than the yarn, it will need to be placed inside a muslin bag or a fine net bag to hold the fibres together. Angora dyes to a lighter value than wool and therefore more dye is needed to dye angora to the same shade as wool.

Commercial yarns

These may still contain spinning oil which has to be removed prior to dyeing. Scour by soaking them in a warm solution of water at 70°C (158°F), and to each litre of water add 1 ml of liquid detergent and 1 ml of ammonia (1 tsp detergent and 1 tsp ammonia to 8 pints of water). Immerse the yarn for 20 minutes then rinse in clear water many times.

Silk

Silk is made up of proteins which are damaged by high temperatures, agitation and strong alkalis. If it is clean and free from gum it is prepared in the same way as for other animal fibres, but any sticky yellow gum has to be removed before dyeing begins.

Make a 1% soap solution by using 5 gm (5 level tsp) of soap flakes added to 500 gm (2 cups) of warm water and stirred until they are dissolved.

Place the silk in a muslin bag and soak it in a bath of hand-hot water for 20 minutes. Remove the silk and for every 1 gm of silk add 30 gm (2 tbsp) of soap solution. Gradually increase the temperature of the bath until it reaches 84°C (185°F) which is just below simmer point. Hold the bath at this temperature for one hour.

The silk is ready for rinsing and dyeing if it feels free of any stickiness. If it does not feel completely clean after the first degumming, it may be given a second bath using half the amount of soap solution, and maintaining top temperature for half an hour, before finally rinsing.

After the silk has been dyed, a little vinegar added to the final rinse water will neutralize any residual alkalis and slightly harden the surface of the silk, making it shine.

Cellulose fabrics

Fabrics such as cotton and linen have been partially scoured prior to weaving but need to be boiled for 30 minutes with a neutral detergent to remove all sizing or starches which may react with the dye. The fabric is then thoroughly rinsed and is ready for dyeing. If the cloth is for batik or any other surface decoration, drying and ironing will follow.

Cellulose yarns or fibres

These often contain waxes or pectins which are more difficult to remove, because the tough fibres are not easy to penetrate. They are usually boiled for one to two hours, depending on the strength of the fibre, in hot water to which detergent and washing soda have been added. Use a quarter the weight of soda to weight of fibre (eg 1 ounce of soda to 4 ounces of fibre, or 25 gm of soda to 100 gm of fibre).

Leave the yarn or fibre in the liquid until it is cold. Rinse the fibre well. It is then ready for mordanting or dyeing.

An alternate recipe for scouring cellulose fibres uses caustic soda instead of washing soda. The yarn is boiled for one to two hours in water containing detergent and caustic soda. Use 15 gm caustic soda with 15 ml liquid detergent to 1 kg of fibre, or 1.5 gm caustic soda with 1.5 ml liquid detergent to 100 gm fibre.

Caustic soda is always **added to** cold water. It needs to be well rinsed out of the fibre for about 15 minutes in warm running water, then gradually cooled in progressively cooling rinses until it is cold. Use rubber gloves to handle caustic soda and avoid splashing this corrosive liquid.

Bleaching of cotton, flax and other cellulose fibres
This takes place after scouring, if required. Use household bleach which is usually sold as 4% sodium hypochlorite solution.

For 100 gm dry fibre use:
3 litres of warm water + 4 ml bleach + 24 gm of washing soda

For 500 gm of dry fibre use:
15 litres of warm water + 19 ml bleach + 120 gm of washing soda

For 1 kg of dry fibre use:
30 litres of warm water + 38 ml bleach + 240 gm of washing soda

Dissolve the soda in a little hot water and add it to the bleach bath. Enter the wet skeins into the solution and turn them occasionally. Leave for 30–45 minutes. Remove the fibre and squeeze out the excess liquid and air the fibre for a few hours before rinsing for five minutes in cold running water.

Man-made fibres
These may contain spinning oils or dirt: washing in hand-hot detergent water is usually sufficient to remove these. If the fibre feels very greasy, a little washing soda may be added to the water. Leave the fibres to soak in the solution for 30–40 minutes before rinsing.

For 100 gm of dry fibre weight use 1 gm of washing soda and 1ml of liquid detergent.

Cool the temperature of the rinse waters very gradually until they are cold, to avoid creasing the fabrics.

EQUIPMENT

We would all like to own a dyehouse with stainless steel benches, plenty of shelving, cupboards that lock, and low stoves for dye pots, but most of us have to work in the kitchen. That is no problem providing that we take all safety precautions. Wherever it is, the work area should be clean, flat, and in good light.

Dye pots and utensils are kept specifically for dyeing. Covering work surfaces with paper which can be burnt after use is an excellent practice, especially when weighing and mixing mordants. I recommend using rubber gloves to protect the hands, especially from mordants and chemicals, and I always use a face mask when handling caustic substances, dusty mordants or powdered dyestuffs.

A set of reliable scales is essential for weighing fibres and dyestuffs.

Dye pots
A pot needs to be large enough to hold the fibre to be dyed and sufficient water to give a good circulation, yet be light enough to lift. A handle is necessary to be able to move it, and a lid is required to reduce condensation and to exclude light from sensitive mordants.

If you dye large amounts of fibre an old boiler with a tap makes dyeing easy. Stainless steel is ideal, because the metal does not react with the dye, and pots

Suitable dye pots

enamelled on the inside are excellent, providing that they are not chipped, exposing bare metal. Secondhand shops may have just the pot you need, but choose carefully. Copper, brass and iron pots react with the metal salts of the mordant and sadden the dyes, and for this reason, although they are easier to acquire, they are best avoided.

Pots should be scoured well at the end of a dye session and rinsed well to remove any traces of abrasive cleaner, because a dirty pot will spoil the next dye. Indigo dye leaves a scum which is difficult to remove and a pot kept especially for vat dyeing is a good idea. Iron mordant eats into pots and I have usually kept an old pot for this mordant.

Equipment for chemical dyeing is similar; it is described more fully in Chapter Three. Instructions and equipment for direct application methods may be found in Chapters Six and Seven.

LIQUOR RATIO

Recipes throughout the book make frequent mention of the **liquor ratio**, which is a guide to the amount of water needed in a dye bath.

The volume of water increases with the weight of the fibre. The liquor ratio is expressed as a ratio of water to weight of the fibre to be dyed. Using the metric system makes this calculation easy because 1 ml of water weighs 1 gm and therefore mls and gms are interchangeable in an equation. In imperial measure 1 fluid oz weighs 1 oz and 1 pint contains 20 fluid ounces.

Most recipes call for a liquor rate of 30:1 (written L/R 30:1). This means that for every 1 gm of fibre 30ml of liquor is used or, in other words, 30 times the

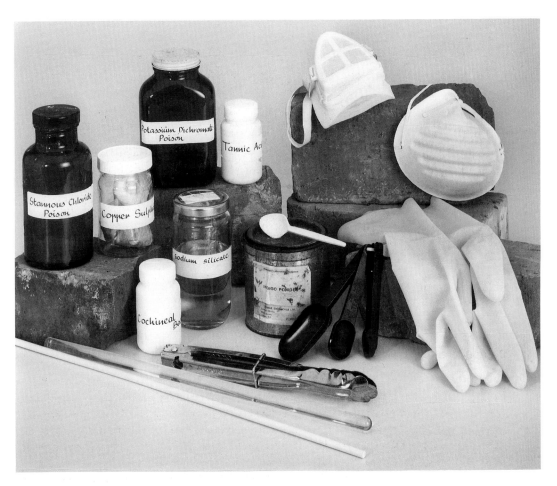

A dyer's tools: well labelled bottles for mordants and chemicals (kept out of reach of children), with a selection of jars and spoons for mixing. Glass rods and stainless steel or plastic spoons to stir the dye or mordant. Wooden dowels, rods and tongs are useful, but need to be replaced when they become stained. Rubber gloves to protect the hands from dyes and mordants, and a disposable face mask to prevent inhalation of fine powders.

For small samples, toughened glass from chemical supply houses are very useful.

weight of water to weight of fibre. Here are some examples of a 30:1 liquor ratio.

To dye:

50 gm of fibre:	30 x 50 = 1,500ml = 1.5 litres of water
100 gm of fibre:	30 x 100 = 3,000ml = 3.0 litres of water
500 gm of fibre:	30 x 500 = 15,000ml = 15.0 litres of water
1 kg of fibre:	30 x 1000 = 30,000ml = 30.0 litres of water

To dye:

1 oz fibre:	30 x 1 = 30 fluid oz = $1^1/2$ pints
8 oz fibre:	30 x 8 = 240 fluid oz = $1^1/2$ gallon
1 lb fibre:	30 x 16 = 480 fluid oz = 3 gallon

This calculation is easy to use and satisfactory for most dye and mordant processes for natural or chemical dyes.

Note that the amount of liquid means the **total** volume, including the liquid in which the dyes and additives are suspended prior to adding them to the dyebath, so make allowances for these.

Bulky fleece fibre may need a liquor ratio of 35:1 or 40:1 to allow sufficient circulation of dye liquid around the fibre, so alter the recipe to this ratio if you think it advisable.

When dyeing small amounts, such as 1 gm of fine yarn, there is rarely sufficient liquid for good circulation, so I use approximately 200 ml of water in a chemical beaker for a small test sample. As the liquid evaporates during dyeing, more is added to maintain the ratio.

Fair Isle jacket in natural coloured and plant dyed wool. Handspun and knitted by Lyall Campbell.

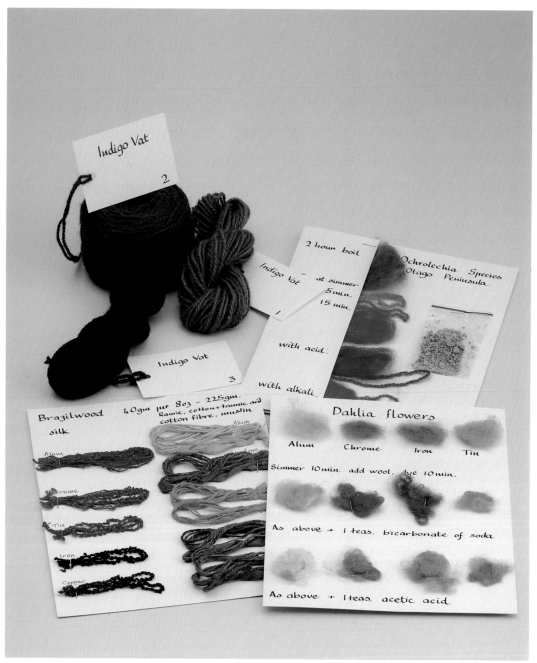

Records can be as simple or as complicated as you wish them to be.

2. NATURAL DYEING

USING NATURAL DYES

There will be unexpected sources of dye materials around you, wherever you live, and the joy of using natural dyes is discovering them for yourself. The aromatic smell of the yarn, and the soft, warm, subtle colours will be your reward.

This year my camellias flowered early in winter. There is always an uncertainty and element of surprise in gardening and it is the same when using vegetable dyes. The soil, altitude, temperature and the amount of rainfall all influence the colour of the dye, and consequently the colours that I have produced in my recipes are intended only as a guide. Lichens that have plenty of rainfall tend to produce richer, deeper shades than those growing in drier areas. Young silver dollar gum leaves cut in the spring are more likely to produce the brick shades than the leaves from older trees cut in the summer.

Keeping records

Because of variations like these it is sensible to keep records of the plants, the time of year that they were picked, and the place and situation in which they grew.

Many people believe that keeping records takes too much time and effort. But they are extremely useful: recording as much relevant information as possible will enable you to match colours, select shades, and to relate dye materials to the season, time of year, and place of origin. They don't have to be beautiful, but keep them clean, out of sunlight, and away from moths! They will be easier to read if they are kept inside polythene covers, and less likely to be lost if they are kept in a file or book.

Storage of dye material

Most dyestuffs are best used fresh, especially flowers, but I do keep a store of dye materials ready for instant use.

Pine cones, tree barks, acorns, walnut shells and onion skins hang in string bags in a cool dry place. Lichens are dried and labelled, and kept in a dry place out of sunlight. Flowers, such as weld, and silver dollar gum leaves are dried and tied in bunches and hung in a dark dry basement. In my freezer there are all manner of things from berries, to leaves and flowers! Frozen materials need to be dropped straight into a hot dye bath to prevent too much deterioration when thawing. The colour is not quite as good as if they had been used fresh, but they are a useful addition to my dyes in the winter. Labelling of dye material is crucial in a freezer.

I also keep a stock of imported dyes and thereby ensure that I have dye material all the year round.

Poisonous dye plants

We are brought up as children to respect hemlock, fungi, poison ivy, bittersweet, and not to eat green potatoes. The native tutu (*Coriaria arborea*) can poison man with convulsions, gastric disorders and finally exhaustion. The yew tree contains poisonous oil, and cherry laurel and ngaio are on the suspected list.

Many berries are poisonous. Bulbs are toxic, and could even be fatal when eaten. Seeds from peach, wild plum, and apple can also be toxic in quantity. You may not eat them but children may try! Animals may take spent dye materials from your garden. (My dog eats all manner of 'throw out' vegetables from my compost heap.) Blackberries, which are not toxic in themselves, may have been sprayed with weedkillers. Nettles irritate the skin and chrome should also be labelled as an irritant.

Basically I think it sound advice to treat all dye stuffs as a potential danger. Wash your hands well after collecting them and wear rubber gloves when dyeing. Keep everything out of the reach of children, especially in the liquid stage when it could be drunk. Bury all remains for complete safety.

In case of an accident, when one of the family for no apparent reason vomits badly, has severe stomach pain or even convulsions, ask yourself if your plants or mordants could be the culprit. Remember what they are, and telephone your doctor or hospital. With a certain amount of care this should never happen to you.

MORDANTING

Some natural dyes require nothing but dye liquor to give a good colour to fibres. These are called **substantive** dyes: lichens and walnut shells are good examples of these.

The majority need a weak solution of metal salts to assist the dye to 'fix' to the fibres. We use the word 'mordant' for these chemical assistants, which comes from the French word *mordre*, meaning 'to bite'. Depending upon which metal salt is used as a mordant, the same dye produces a range of colours. You can dye and mordant simultaneously, but pre-mordanting gives brighter results, especially when using an alum mordant. Mordanting is the most important part of dyeing because unlevel mordant gives an unlevel dye.

Cover the scales with paper before weighing the mordant. Put on your rubber gloves, and cover your work surfaces.

Rotate the fibre very slowly during the process to ensure even take-up of the mordant. Vigorous movement or rapid boiling will felt animal fibres.

Leave the fibre to cool in the mordant, then gently remove it and rinse it in warm water. Roll it in a towel and keep it until required.

Fibre treated with an alum mordant is best kept for three days before dyeing. The others may be dyed immediately.

Mordanting silk
Silk dyes to a darker shade than cellulose fibres but is a little less vivid than wool. Use the same amount of mordant as you would for a medium wool fibre, but mordant for 1 hour, leave the fibre to cool in the liquid, and steep for 12 hours. The temperature for silk must not rise above 84°C, 185°F or the silk will become damaged. This temperature is a little below simmer point.

After mordanting and dyeing do not squeeze or wring the fibre dry. White silk yarn, *Bombyx mori*, is rolled in a towel to remove excess moisture, then the skein is pulled sharply to straighten the fibres. White silk is ironed while still wet for the best results. Wild tussah silk which is yellower in colour, can be stretched to dry. Press it only when dry.

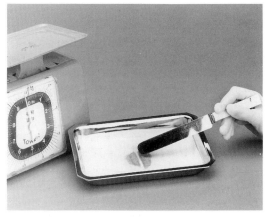

Some amounts of mordant used in the recipes are so small that they are difficult to weigh. Measure 1 ounce or 25 gm, and divide this into portions.

Mix the mordant thoroughly with hot water and when completely dissolved add it to a bath of cold water and stir well.

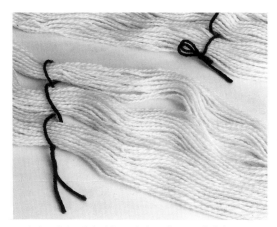

A skein of wool tied *loosely* in a figure of eight to allow penetration of the dye or the mordant liquor. A tie that is too tight acts as a resist and you will have an undyed patch as a result.

Add the wet fibre and very slowly bring the water to boiling point. Simmer for 45 minutes or 1 hour for coarse fibres.

Mordanting and dyeing cellulose fibres

Natural dye colours are not so intense on cellulose fibres as they are on animal fibres and, with a few exceptions, they produce very pale shades. However, they are very beautiful, and I suggest that any good depth of dye on wool is worth trying on cellulose fibres.

I tested imported dyes on ramie, bleached linen, flax and cotton yarns and fabrics. For best results I increased the mordant-to-fibre ratio by three times the amount given (known as **triple mordanting**), though for large amounts of fibre this is an expensive exercise. After mordanting, cellulose fibres are left to steep in the solution for 12–24 hours.

Natural dyes are much stronger on cellulose fibres if they have been subjected to a tannic acid bath before mordanting. The acid assists the mordant fixation to the fibre, therefore improving the washfast qualities of the dye. Tannic acid is easy to use and is obtainable from a chemist or drugstore. It comes in powder form and does not damage the fibre, although after a tannic acid bath the fibre is very slightly browned.

Tannic acid bath

For every 100 gm of fibre use 6 gm of tannic acid (1 ounce of tannic acid for every 1 lb of fibre). Dissolve the tannic acid in a little hot water. Prepare the bath with 5 litres of water to each 100 gm of fibre (10 pints to each 4 ounces). Add the acid solution then enter the wet fibre.

Slowly raise the temperature to boiling point then reduce it to simmer. Maintain this temperature for 30 minutes. Remove the bath from the heat source.

Leave the fibre to steep in the liquid for 24 hours. After rinsing the fibre is ready for mordanting.

THE MORDANTS

Alum (potassium aluminium sulphate)

This is the most commonly used mordant because it is non-toxic and can be bought cheaply at most chemists or drugstores. Cream of tartar is used in combination with alum to help brighten the colour.

For every 100 gm of wool use:
19 gm of alum for fine/medium wool *or* 25 gm of alum for medium/coarse wool *and* 6 gm of cream of tartar

For 1 kg of wool use:
187 gm of alum for fine/medium wool *or* 250 gm of alum for medium/coarse wool
and 62 gm of cream of tartar

For 1 lb of wool use:
3 oz of alum for fine/medium wool *or* 4 oz of alum for medium/coarse wool
and 1 oz of cream of tartar

The wool will be sticky to handle if you use too much alum. Although it is possible to dye immediately after mordanting, you will get brighter colours if you remove the fibre from the mordant bath, roll it into a towel, and keep it for three days before dyeing. This will allow the alum to penetrate the fibres fully.

Chrome (dichromate of potash)

This mordant is sensitive to light and must be kept in a dark place. The dye pot should have a lid to exclude the light. When mordanting is finished, the fibre can be dyed immediately, or it may be washed and rolled into a towel to keep it dark until required for dyeing.

Our skin is very sensitive to chrome mordant, so please remember to use rubber gloves. It is also a poison and therefore needs careful handling.

Chrome mordant leaves wool soft to handle, but too much mordant will impair the dye colour. Use the lesser amounts given for fine to medium fibres and the greater amount for coarser fibre.

For 100 gm of fibre use : 1.5–3 gm of chrome
For 1 kg of fibre use: 15–30 gm of chrome
For 1 lb of fibre use: $^1/4$–$^1/2$ oz of chrome

Iron (ferrous sulphate)

I keep a special pot for this mordant because it gradually eats away at the metal, which could spoil a subsequent dye. Weigh iron carefully because too much will make the fibre hard. Iron also needs to be thoroughly dissolved, or it will mordant unevenly. It is inexpensive and can be purchased from a drugstore or chemist. If swallowed by a child it could be fatal, so keep well out of children's reach.

For 100 gm of wool use: 3 gm of ferrous sulphate and 6 gm of cream of tartar
For 1 kg of wool use: 31 gm of ferrous sulphate and 62 gm of cream of tartar
For 1 lb of wool use: $^1/2$ oz ferrous sulphate and 1 oz of cream of tartar

Tin (stannous chloride)

This mordant is a poison and needs to be treated with respect. As it is also expensive, you will only wish to buy a small amount at a time. It comes in the form of crystals which are difficult to dissolve, and you will need to dissolve them in boiling water before adding them to the mordant bath. Too much tin makes the wool very brittle.

After hearing about all of the difficulties and the care needed, you will wonder why I bother with it at all, but tin is used when bright shades of reds, oranges and yellows, are sought.

Weigh the tin carefully and after mordanting rinse the fibre really well to make sure that all traces of it have been removed. The fibre is ready to dye directly after mordanting.

Some dyers add the tin mordant at the end of the dye bath stage, but I have found that pre-mordanting gives brighter shades.

For 100 gm of wool use: 3 gm of stannous chloride and 13 gm of cream of tartar
For 1 kg of wool use: 31 gm of stannous chloride and 125 gm of cream of tartar
For 1 lb of wool use: $^1/2$ oz of stannous chloride and 2 oz of cream of tartar

Dissolve the cream of tartar in water and add it to the mordant bath first, then dissolve the tin in boiling water and add it to the bath. Oxalic acid may be substituted for cream of tartar, using the same amount.

Copper sulphate

This mordant does not have the scope of previous ones but if the plant yields a green dye, this mordant will find it. It is easy to obtain from garden shops and chemists. It does not cost very much and is a useful addition to a list of mordants.

For 100 gm of wool use: 3 gm of copper sulphate

For 1 kg of wool use: 30 gm of copper sulphate
For 1 lb of wool use: $^1/_2$ oz of copper sulphate

ACIDS AND ALKALIS

Some amazing changes can be made to a dye by adding an acid or alkali, and a little experimentation often proves worthwhile. After the fibre has been dyed, remove it from the dye pot. Add the acid or alkali to the dye liquor and stir well before re-entering the fibre. You may prefer to tip some of the dye liquor into another vessel in order to do a small test dye. If you are really investigating the potential of a dye, use two pots and add an acid to one and an alkali to the other.

Alkalis include bicarbonate of soda, ammonia, soap powder.

Acids include acetic acid (vinegar is approximately 4% acetic acid), cream of tartar, citric acid.

For 500gm (or 1 lb) of fibre add:
10 gm (2 tsp) of sodium bicarbonate or baking soda
or 15 ml (1 tbsp) of vinegar

Soap powders and abrasives are alkali and may alter dye colours. It is therefore important to remove all traces of them after cleaning the dye pot. Some colours from berry dyes actually change from purple to green when the fibre is washed in soap.

DYEING PROCEDURE

This is the part that you have been waiting for – the element of surprise or the rewarding colour. It is the easiest part of the whole dyeing process.

Weigh the fibre or fabric to be dyed, as this will affect the quantity of dye material required and the amount of water used.

Choose your dye material. If it is going to tangle in the fibres during dyeing, wrap it up first in a muslin cloth. It should equal the weight of the fibre, with the exception of leaves, which I usually double.

I do not add salt to my dyes since my tests show that if a dye is going to fade, the addition of salt does not change the outcome. One exception to this is that I do use salt when dyeing cotton or linen with cochineal.

Select your dye pot and add sufficient water to cover the fibre and allow free circulation. You may either put your mordanted fibre and dyestuff in the dye pot together and slowly extract the colour and dye simultaneously, or you may extract the dye from the dyestuff, allow the liquor to cool, remove the dye material and enter the wetted fibre to proceed with the dye. In both cases bring the temperature very slowly to boiling point then reduce the temperature to simmer. Over-boiling reduces the brilliance of a colour.

The colour of the liquid is no indication of the dye colour. When fibre is wet, it appears darker in colour than when dry. To get an idea of the final shade, squeeze a portion of the fibre between your fingers to remove some of the liquid.

Dye sufficient fibre to complete your project and add a little extra as a safety measure, because it is almost impossible to reproduce a dye shade exactly.

Bundles of leaves tied with string ready for the dye pot.

Flowers tied in muslin to stop them tangling with the fibre to be dyed.

Use glass rods or clean dowels to rotate the fibre gently once or twice to ensure even dyeing: the dye will take faster in the hot spots of your dye pot and the fibre could be quite dark near the base of the pot and very pale near the surface. If you move animal fibres too vigorously through hot liquids they will felt, and any sudden changes in temperature between dye and rinse water will damage the ends of the fibre. Felting of the cut end of a staple of fleece after dyeing is a very common but avoidable problem for spinners.

Rinse the fibre very gently after dyeing, to remove all traces of dye liquid and mordant. Skeins of yarn may be rolled in a towel to remove excess moisture, then threaded on to a length of muslin and hung on the washing line to dry. Fleeces or other fibres may be wrapped in muslin and given a short, gentle spin dry in a washing machine before drying. Never put animal fibres into a dryer or they will felt horribly. The fibres will dry quite quickly in a gentle breeze.

SOLAR DYEING

Instead of using conventional heat sources to cook natural dye liquids, you can use the heat rays from the sun. This method is slower, but you can see the dyes develop. Many dyers state that the wool is softer when solar dyed, because there is no friction from the boiling process. The colours will be more delicate in cooler climates but in warmer areas the shades should be equal to those from conventionally heated dyes.

You will need a clear glass container to attract the rays. (Coloured glass or plastic containers are not suitable.) It must be large enough to give a really good circulation of dye liquid, because crammed fibre dyes very unevenly. The ideal top for the container is glass, but a plastic seal anchored with an elastic band is a good substitute.

The dye material is used in a ratio of at least an equal weight of material to fibre, and preferably double the weight for good results. Hard, dry dyestuffs such as pine cones, acorns, twigs or barks, may be soaked for a few days before they are used. For the best results the dye is extracted from the material first. Simmer the dye material in water for as long as the recipes state necessary to extract colour. For flowers and plants this is usually about 20–30 minutes. Strain the liquid and into this dissolve the carefully weighed mordant.

The wool must be well washed to remove the grease and must be wet when put into the container. This reduces the number of bubbles in the dye liquid and aids even dyeing. Pour the dye/mordant liquid over the fibre and shake it to remove any extra air bubbles. Cover the container with a glass lid or plastic wrap to seal the jar. Place this in a sunny position for a minimum of 10 days, and a maximum of one month – depending upon how many warm sunny days you have had. Shake or stir the fibre inside the container every day.

Premordanted wool may be used instead of adding the mordant to the dye liquor if you wish.

Another method of solar dyeing is to layer wool and dyestuff in the container and to pour warm water, in which the mordant has been dissolved, over the fibre. Seal it and proceed in the usual manner. This is more suitable for small quantities of fibre because each container of dye will produce a slightly different shade.

Solar dyeing

NATURAL DYE RECIPES

The following dye recipes are the result of my own experimentation and represent a very small proportion of available dye material. The recipe gives the **simmer** time for dye extraction and the **dye** time. Remember that if you enter dyestuff and fibre together you will need to add the times together to give total time for immersion.

The **mordant** is given in the left column with the resulting shade with comment, where necessary, below. All of the dyes listed here have been ruthlessly tested for fading.

Dyes marked *   have faded slightly
Dyes marked **   have faded to an unsatisfactory degree

Dyeing with flowers
Use the same weight of dyestuff as weight of fibre to be dyed. Pick them when they are fresh and use them as soon as possible.

Acacia riciana
Simmer 10 minutes / dye 20 minutes

Alum	lemon yellow *
Chrome	gamboge yellow
Iron	grey green
Tin	daffodil yellow *

All acacias or wattles give colour.

Broom *(Sarothamnus scoparius)*
Simmer 20 minutes / dye 10 minutes

Alum	pale yellow **
Chrome	buff yellow
Iron	pale grey
Tin	pale yellow

Buddleia royal davidii
Simmer 20 minutes / dye 20 minutes

Alum	acid yellow
Chrome	lime yellow
Iron	soft olive
Tin	grass green

This is a red purple variety.
Purple flowers dye yellow.

Cineraria
Simmer 15 minutes / dye 30 minutes

Alum	off white
Chrome	pale yellow green
Iron	silver grey
Tin	pale lemon **

Chrysanthemum
Simmer 10 minutes / dye 15 minutes

Alum	lemon
Chrome	strong yellow
Iron	green grey
Tin	strong lemon

Darker flowers give a greater depth of colour.

Dahlia
Simmer 10 minutes / dye 10 minutes

Alum	gamboge * (1)
Chrome	rust red * (2)
Iron	olive * (3)
Tin	flame orange *

(1) Apricot shade with alkali.
(2) Deeper shade with alkali.
(3) Darker flowers give a greater depth of colour.

Dandelion (Taraxacum officinale)
Simmer 20 minutes / dye 20 minutes

Alum	lemon
Chrome	gamboge
Iron	grey green
Tin	bright lemon **

Flax (Phormium tenax)
Simmer 20 minutes / dye 20 minutes

Alum	beige brown
Chrome	chestnut
Iron	pink beige
Tin	golden chestnut

Use the flowers in bud. Stalks give a paler colour but it fades.

Foxglove (Digitalis purpurea)
Simmer 15 minutes / dye 20 minutes

Alum	lemon
Chrome	gold
Iron	green grey
Tin	brilliant yellow

Flowers and stalks used.

Gorse (Ulex europæus)
Simmer 10 minutes / dye 15 minutes

Alum	lemon
Chrome	gold
Iron	green
Tin	orange yellow **

Grape hyacinth (Muscari)
Simmer 30 minutes / dye 30 minutes

Alum	pale blue **
Chrome	pale blue **
Iron	no colour
Tin	blue **

Hypericum (H. leschenaultii)
Simmer 15 mins / dye 20 mins

Alum	cream
Chrome	pale yellow
Iron	pale grey
Tin	yellow **

Marigold (Tagetes erecta)
15 minutes / dye 30 minutes

Alum	cream *
Chrome	pale apple green
Iron	soft grey
Tin	soft lemon *

Nerine
Simmer 10 minutes / dye 20 minutes

Alum	little colour
Chrome	apple green *
Iron	grey *
Tin	teal green *

Pelargonium
Simmer 20 minutes / dye 30 minutes

Alum	pale yellow
Chrome	strong green
Iron	dark grey
Tin	ochre yellow

Dark flowers were used.

Tree fuchsia (Fuchsia excorticata)
Simmer 20 minutes / dye 20 minutes

Alum	soft lemon
Chrome	yellow green
Iron	dark grey
Tin	lemon *

Red flowers used here.

Berries and fruits for dyeing

Although berries produce beautiful shades, they are the most likely to fade in sunlight. Another factor to consider is that most berries are acidic and the purpley colour they produce can be changed and lost when subjected to alkalis such as soap powders, natural sheep suint, ammonia or bicarbonate of soda. Another surprise is that some bright red berries give practically no colour at all!

Wrap berries in muslin and crush them while they are simmering to extract as much colour as possible. Woody fruits such as pine cones, acorns and walnut shells need to be crushed, and hot water is poured over them initially. They are then left in the water for 2–4 days and the liquid plus the dye material is used for the dye bath.

Acorns (*Quercus*)

Simmer 30 minutes / dye 60 minutes

Alum	buff
Chrome	dark olive
Iron	deep purple grey
Tin	yellow ochre

Leave to steep for several days before using.

Blackberries (*Rubus fruiticosus*)

Simmer 20 minutes / dye 20 minutes

Alum	pink **
Chrome	grey **
Iron	grey **
Tin	purple **

Pinks change to greens with the addition of alkalis, but they also fade.

Pine cones (*Pinus radiata*)

Simmer 2 hours / dye 45 minutes

Alum	pale beige
Chrome	soft yellow brown
Iron	pale grey brown
Tin	light tan

Elderberries (*Sambucus nigra*)

Simmer 20 minutes / dye 20 minutes

Alum	soft purple *
Chrome	soft purple *
Iron	soft purple **
Tin	strong violet *

In an aluminium pot, alum and bicarbonate of soda give a soft green. Add soap and it darkens. Sadly, the colours fade.

Tree tomatoes (*Cyphomandra betacea*)

Simmer 20 mins / dye 15 mins

Alum	grey **
Chrome	blue grey **
Iron	grey **
Tin	blue **

Walnut shells (*Juglans regia*)

Simmer 30 minutes / dye 60 minutes

Alum	straw
Chrome	yellow olive
Iron	mid brown
Tin	tan

Soak for 4 days before using or for 4–6 days for darker shades. No mordant produces pink beige.

Roots

Use the same weight of roots as weight of fibre to be dyed. Wash the roots before you begin to dye.

Beetroot globes (Beta vulgaris)

Simmer 30 minutes / dye 60 minutes

Alum	soft apricot **
Chrome	deep straw **
Iron	soft apricot **
Tin	pale tan *

These lovely shades fade very quickly.

Dock root (Rumex obtusifolius)

Simmer 15 minutes / dye 60 minutes

Alum	yellow brown
Chrome	chestnut
Iron	mid brown
Tin	yellow brown

Cleaver roots (Galium aparine)

Simmer 30 minutes / dye 90 minutes

Alum	pinky salmon
Chrome	brownish purple
Iron	beige
Tin	salmon orange

Use an aluminium dye pot. The fine roots, which are related to madder, are difficult to collect.

Flax roots (Phormium tenax)

Simmer 90 minutes / dye 60 minutes

Alum	red brown
Chrome	dark chocolate
Iron	red brown
Tin	chestnut

Tree barks

If you ringbark a tree it will die, so your first consideration is where to find tree bark that does not need to be stripped from the tree. A felled tree is a natural choice. Some botanical gardens are most co-operative. I have used bark from firewood with some success. Some fuchsias and eucalyptus trees naturally shed their bark.

To dye with bark use the same weight of dyestuff as weight of fibre. Break the bark into small pieces, tie them into muslin and immerse them in the dye bath and leave them to soak for 24 hours. Use the liquid and the bark for dyeing.

Blue gum (Eucalyptus globulus)

Simmer 2 hours / dye 1 hour

Alum	brown
Chrome	bronze green
Iron	vandyke brown
Tin	straw

Eucalyptus produce a wide variety of colours including reds, yellows, greens and browns.

Coprosma grandiflora

Simmer 1 hour / dye 1 hour

Alum	vandyke brown
Chrome	very dark brown
Iron	lovat green
Tin	chestnut

In an aluminium pot without a mordant add soda to give a dull red. Add tin crystals to brighten.

Elder bark (Sambucus nigra)

Simmer 2 hours / dye 90 minutes

Alum	cream *
Chrome	cream
Iron	pale grey
Tin	pale straw *

Macrocarpa (Cupressus macrocarpa)

Simmer 2 hours / dye 30 minutes

Alum	pale beige*
Chrome	dark cream*
Iron	pale grey*
Tin	dark cream*

Tanekaha (Phyllocladus trichomanoides)

Simmer 1 hour / dye 1 hour

Alum	dusky pink
Chrome	rust red
Iron	brown
Tin	orange red

Willow (Salix triandra)

Simmer 1 hour / dye 1 hour

Alum	beige**
Chrome	pale brown
Iron	dark straw
Tin	straw**

Rhus twigs (Cotinus coggygria folis purpureis)

Simmer 1 hour / dye 15 mins

Alum	bright yellow (1)
Chrome	orange red (2)
Iron	green (3)
Tin	vivid orange (4)

(1) With soda gives apricot.
(2) With soda gives rust red.
(3) With soda gives chestnut.
(4) Darkens with soda.

Leaves as dye materials

Use fresh leaves and in a generous proportion. I suggest twice the weight of leaves to weight of fibre.

Blackberry shoots (Rubus fruticosus)

Simmer 30 minutes / dye 20 minutes

Alum	pale apple green
Chrome	bright apple green
Iron	purple brown
Tin	soft yellow

Collect them when they are very young.

Blue gum (Eucalyptus globulus)

Simmer 30 minutes / dye 15 minutes

Alum	straw
Chrome	gold
Iron	purple brown
Tin	mustard

Results are from using winter leaves. Summer leaves give lighter shades.

Bracken buds (Pteridium esculentum)

Simmer 2 hours / dye 2 hours

Alum	beige
Chrome	tan
Iron	grey
Tin	yellow tan

Dodonea viscosa purpurea

Simmer 20 minutes / dye 30 minutes

Alum	pale green *
Chrome	yellow green *
Iron	beige grey *
Tin	bright green

Elder leaves (Sambucus ebulus)

Simmer 30 minutes / dye 30 minutes

Alum	pale yellow **
Chrome	strong yellow
Iron	grey
Tin	yellow

Parsley (Petroselinum crispum)

Simmer 20 minutes / dye 30 minutes

Alum	off white
Chrome	lime green
Iron	little colour
Tin	pale yellow

Use four times the weight of parsley to weight of fibre.

Flowering Cherry (Prunus cerasus)

Simmer 20 minutes / dye 20 minutes

Alum	soft yellow green **
Chrome	yellow green
Iron	grey **
Tin	gold

Use the red bronze leaves from most flowering cherries.

Cotinus coggygria

Simmer 30 minutes / dye 30 minutes

Alum	pale green grey
Chrome	olive
Iron	purple grey
Tin	grass green *

This is the bronze-leaved smoke bush.

Silver dollar gum leaves (Eucalyptus cinerea)

Simmer 2 hours / dye 1 hour

Alum	red
Chrome	brick red
Iron	wine
Tin	brick red

Initial dyeing gives pale yellow greens. Reds need time to extract.

Onion skins (Allium cepa)

Simmer 15 minutes / dye 10 minutes

Alum	strong yellow
Chrome	orange gold
Iron	bronze brown
Tin	orange yellow

Blue tree scale or Gum tree scale (Eriococcus coriaceus)

These tiny legless insects may be found on the lower leaves and branches of eucalyptus trees. They have light brown bodies with a small hole at one end and a cream brown underside. They are almost hollow, but contain a powerful carmine dye. I look for them in late spring and early summer. Their life cycle is very short and they dry off towards the end of it. They are not easy to collect because it is important to scrape away any eucalyptus which may spoil the dye.

   The colour they give will depend upon the amount of liquid they contain and whether or not they have become infested by a small parasitic wasp. The maroon colour on unmordanted fibre will fade, but the vivid reds and oranges obtained with tin mordant and cream of tartar appear to be colour fast. I have also achieved a bright orange using alum and cream of tartar as a mordant. Do not throw away the dye until you have tried second and third exhausts which give paler apricots and pale corals.

DYEING WITH LICHENS

A lichen is composed of a fungus and algae cells living together as one, and when a piece is broken off you can see the two layers. The fungal part is white and the algae is green or blue green. They also produce 'lichen acids' which are not found in other plants, and the dominant acid has a bearing upon the colour obtained as a dye. Usnic acid will dye yellow but the presence of a stronger acid may suppress it. Boiling the lichens in water extracts dyes which mainly produce shades of fawn, brown and orange. Although mordants can be used to 'lift' or deepen a colour, they make little difference to these substantive dyes.

A lichen takes many years to reproduce and for this reason a collector must be responsible for the conservation of these plants. Take only the required amount, from an area with an abundance of that lichen. If there is insufficient for your needs, look elsewhere, or come back in 60 years!

Lichens grow on rocks, trees, or on the ground. They are easier to gather after rain when they are more swollen, and in calm weather when they will not blow away. I use a sharp scraper, and hold a paper bag beneath as I gather them, so as not to waste any. If not required immediately, they may be dried very slowly in the sun or in a very cool oven, and stored in airtight containers until needed. Any mould growing on them in storage will kill the colour-giving properties.

A stronger colour will be given by a lichen growing in a sunny aspect, than a similar lichen growing in the shade, and those receiving adequate rainfall produce better shades than those receiving less.

There are two ways of extracting dyes from lichens. The boiling method is the most commonly used, or the lichens containing lecanoric or gyrophoric acid can be steeped in ammonia or urine to extract reds and magentas.

Boiling method

Bruise and soak the lichen in water for 24 hours after removing and discarding any bark or moss. Use the same weight of lichen as fibre to be dyed. The lichen may be simmered alone for two hours to extract the dye liquor, or put into a muslin and placed on top of the fibre in the dye pot and both simmered together for two hours. Another method is to alternate layers of lichen and fibre and simmer together. The loose lichen shakes free after the fibre is dried. To extract a deeper shade the fibre may be left in the dye overnight without any heat.

Extracting the orchils

A few lichens contain lecanoric acid or gyrophoric acid. These acids are known as the orchil acids, and are very potent. They are only slightly soluble in water, but will react with either urine or ammonia to become soluble organic salts which in turn produce vivid magenta and carmine dyes. They have been used for many years. In Scotland the preparation of locally grown orchil-bearing lichen was known as cudbear, and chalk was added to form a powder. The Dutch made a similar preparation known as litmus, and the French produced orselle d'auvergne. Today we use ammonia, with water and oxygen, and keep the temperature of the preparation between 12–20°C (56–75°F).

Break the lichens into tiny pieces, removing any extraneous matter. Put the lichen pieces into a glass or polythene bottle and cover with one part ammonia to two parts of luke-warm water. Stopper the bottle, but not too tightly, leaving some air space. If in the initial stages of swelling, the lichen absorbs all or most of the liquid, add a little more. The mixture needs to be stirred but fairly thick.

Shake the liquid daily and keep it warm. (I use the airing cupboard above my hot water cylinder.) For rich reds and vivid magentas, leave the liquid for 28 days. A more puce colour is obtained by using the liquor at around 18 days. If there is no red colour in the liquid at 18 days, you may be fairly sure that the lichen does not contain the orchil acids.

At the end of 28 days the fibre may be placed in the cold liquor and left overnight to absorb the colour. Next day I use heat to speed the dyeing. One tablespoon of dye mixture will dye at least 56 gm (2 oz) of fibre, and may be used several times before exhausted. Add water to the dye mixture, enter wet fibre and bring slowly to the boil, then reduce to a simmer for 10–15 minutes. The residue of the dye mixture can be dried and stored for future use.

Lecanoric acid appears to be more lightfast than gyrophoric orchil. When exposed to severe prolonged sunlight there is some loss of colour, but if treated well both should compare with the lightfast qualities of many chemical dyes of similar colour. Wool premordanted with tin seems to retain its colour to a greater degree.

The addition of alkali to the red dye neutralizes it and it becomes purple. The addition of acetic acid or vinegar will change purple to red. Weaker baths that are beginning to exhaust produce pale pinks with alkali, and rusty tans and pink tans with acid.

Here are two ways in which to test for the presence of orchil acids. The simplest is to break the lichen and apply a drop of household bleach containing sodium hypochlorite to the broken edge with the tip of a needle. If it turns red almost immediately, the acids are present. The second method is by trial and error with records. Lichens which do not contain orchil acids often produce wonderful colours by the usual boiling method.

THE LICHENS

Lichens are not easy to classify, especially to anyone with little botanical experience. I suggest that you obtain from your library an illustrated book on lichens in your country. You will initially see that they fall into three main types: crustaceous, foliose and fruticose lichens.

Each lichen has an upper and lower side, and circular or disc-like fruiting bodies which vary in colour from one lichen to another. By matching your lichen to an illustration with a simple description it is possible to be fairly sure of the genus of your lichen. Detailed classification, I leave to the expert. I keep my lichen samples in a small see-through packet attached to my record of the dye, and a note of the place where I found the lichen.

Opposite, top: Crustaceous lichen *Ochrolechria* species. Crustaceous lichens form a very thin crust on rocks, barks, or even soil.
Opposite, bottom: Foliose lichen *Parmelia conspersa.* These are the most abundant, thicker, leafier lichens.

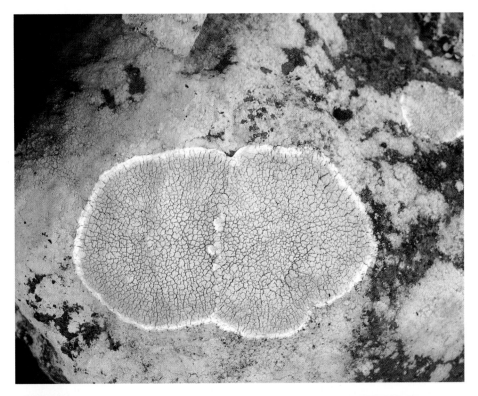

Fruticose lichens *Usnea* species. These are shrubby lichens resembling tufts, as they are held near to the base from which the remainder of the lichen branches. 'Old Man's Beard' is an example.

Crustaceous lichens adhere to rocks like a crust, and these have the orchil acids. They are difficult to classify. Here are three examples I was unable to name:

A white mealy lichen with grey spores
Orchil testing gives magenta.
The addition of bicarbonate of soda deepens the colour, and vinegar changes magenta to red.
Boiling for 2 hours gives mid brown.

A brown fawn lichen with pink spores
Orchil testing gives puce pink within 10 minutes.
Alkali deepens the colour, and vinegar changes it to red.
Boiling for 2 hours gives fawn brown.

A dark grey black lichen with black fruiting bodies
Orchil testing produces vivid magenta within a few minutes. Maximum colour in 15 minutes.
Alkali lightened the colour and acid (vinegar) gave a claret red.
Boiling for 2 hours gives fawn brown.

Other lichens

Baeomyces fungoides
A crustose lichen found on clay banks. It has a pink red fruiting body on a white stalk.
Boiling method gives no colour.
Orchil testing with extra acid added to the dye bath gives a pale salmon.

Cladia retipora
Also known as coral lichen or lace lichen.
Perforations in the stems of this white or grey fruticose lichen give it a lace-like appearance.
Boiling method gives gold.
No orchil present.

Cladonia cornutoradiata
This fruticose lichen is often found on peaty soils. It has thin, round, erect white stems.
Boiling method gives pale lemon.
No orchil present.

Cladonia chlorophaea
A fruticose lichen with round, white, erect stems that open out into a trumpet shape.
Boiling method gives yellow.
No orchil present.

Cladonia mitis
A very small fruticose lichen with thin branches that tangle to form a mass.
Boiling method gives beige.
No orchil present.

Neuropogon ciliata
A fruticose lichen with tough green stems, and branches that are black on top as though burnt by fire.
Boiling method gives a strong tan.
No orchil present.

Parmelia conspersa
A bright yellow green foliose lichen with a black underside. It grows outwards, the outside looking leafy and the centre looking mealy.
Boiling method gives gold tan.
Orchil testing gives a drab apricot.

Parmelia omphalodes
A dark grey brown foliose lichen with a black underside.
Boiling method gives rusty red.
No orchil present.

Parmelia panniformis
A black foliose lichen
Boiling method gives buff.
No orchil present.

Parmelia perlata
A grey green foliose lichen with a black underside.
Boiling method gives rich chestnut.
Orchil testing gives pale pink.

Parmelia reticulata
A green foliose lichen with a black underside and, in parts, mealy looking.
Boiling method gives orange brown.
Orchil testing gives dusky pink, which is brightened with alkali.

Pseudocyphellaria carsoloma

A green, fingerlike lichen with black fruiting bodies around the margins and a black underside.
Boiling method gives tan.
No orchil present.

Pseudocyphellaria colensoi

A foliose lichen not unlike *coronata*. Green when wet and brown when dry, with small fringed margins of outgrowths.
Boiling method continued over several days gives green.
Orchil testing gives yellow which browns with acid.

Pseudocyphellaria flavicans

A foliose lichen, which is yellow when wet and yellow brown when dry. It has distinct clusters of outgrowths on the upper surface and is black or brown on the underside. It resembles *P. colensoi*.
Boiling method gives strong yellows.
Orchil testing gives lemon yellow.

Pseudocyphellaria fossulata

A large, flat, branching, finger-like lichen with brown fruiting bodies on the margins. Pale green when dry.
Boiling method gives beige.
No orchil present.

Pseudocyphellaria foveolata

A branching, foliose, grey green lichen with large black saucer-shaped fruiting bodies.
Boiling method gives tan.
Orchil testing gives pale yellow brown.

Pseudocyphellaria homeophylla

A green brown foliose lichen with narrow lobes with leafy branches. Fruiting bodies are white and small, on the margins.
Boiling method gives deep chestnut.
No orchil present.

Pseudocyphellaria mougeotiana

A brown foliose lichen with leafy margins which curl to show yellow.
Boiling method gives lemon yellow.
No orchil present.

Ramalina menziesii

A shrubby, fruticose lichen with long, pale green, flattened stems, found on fruit trees and fence posts. It has scattered marginal, white, saucer-shaped fruiting bodies.
Boiling method gives light straw colour.
No orchil present.

Stereocaulon corticatulum

A tight, shrubby looking fruticose lichen, grey green in colour with hollow white stems.
Boiling method gives light tans. No orchil present.

Sticta filix

A leafy, branching, foliose lichen growing from a basal stalk. It is green brown when dry.
Boiling method gives dull yellow. No orchil present.

Teloschistes velifer

A bright orange lichen growing in small tufts on rocks, old trees and fence posts.
Boiling method gives buff brown.
Orchil testing gives a pink within 10 minutes. Acid deepens the shade, and bicarbonate of soda gives a pink purple, which when left in sunlight turns slate blue.

Usnea (Old Man's Beard)

Bright green, shrubby, and foliose. It hangs from trees and posts. Others in the same species give a range of colours from chocolate brown to straw.
Boiling method gives bright orange tan.
No orchil present.

Umbilicaria papulosa

A flat, wide lobed black lichen with a grey underside. It is foliose with a central holdfast and the surface appears blistery.
Boiling method gives light brown.
Orchil testing gives magenta.

Xanthoria parietina

A bright yellow fruticose lichen found on fruit trees. It has an off-white underside and circular orange or brown fruiting bodies.
Boiling method gives buff yellow.
Orchil testing gives salmon pink if kept at warm temperature.

Pseudocyphellaria coronata (Sticta coronata)

Some biologists accept *coronata* and *hirta* as the same species. This lichen is yellow in colour, growing in large strips or sheets resembling leather. The underside shows black fruiting bodies. Acetone (nail polish remover) or ether, distinguishes *coronata* from similar looking lichens. One drop on the thallus (main body) turns to a red patch immediately.

This lichen is very interesting because it produces a wide range of colours. The dye liquid is potent and can be used many times before it exhausts, and the colours change as lichen acids are reduced. It appears to have a complex number of lichen acids. There are several ways to produce the extensive colour range.

1. Break the lichen into pieces, add heat and dark purple mauves are released, which exhaust to pink mauve. The boiling method takes only 15 minutes to produce a strong colour. Acid blackens the dye; alkali strengthens the purples.
2. Do not break the lichen. Add hot, but not boiling water and a little ammonia. This produces pinks, corals and apricots with tin, lavender with chrome. Place the lichen in the dye pot and add 1 teaspoon of ammonia to each litre of liquid, and leave it to steep for 10 minutes. The liquid should be red and will give good colour in 10–15 minutes, and deeper rose shades in 1–2 hours. Tin mordant produces corals in 15–30 minutes, and mahogany in 1–2 hours. Acid turns this colour from red to red brown.
3. Use the exhausted form of (2). Break it to release yellow, fawns and greens. Copper encourages greens, iron produces shades of tan, fawn and brown. Acid dulls these to greys or browns.
4. Addition of acetic acid in the form of vinegar shifts the colours.
5. Different mordants will widen the range.

This lichen is so versatile that it is in danger of becoming exploited commercially. It is illegal to take lichens from New Zealand national parks where it grows in tantalizing abundance. Purchase it only from reputable responsible people who collect it from outside these protected areas.

FOREIGN DYESTUFFS

I have given these dyestuffs this title because they are not indigenous to New Zealand. For many years they have been imported by dyers to produce colours not obtainable from locally acquired dye material. This short selection of dyes enables me to cover the crimson, red, black and blue shades so often lacking in the natural dye range. The dyes are strong in depth of colour and useful for overdyeing in conjunction with local dyes. The range can also be extended by using these imported dyes in lesser proportions, to produce delicate pastel shades.

Triple mordanting for cellulose fibres was discussed on p. 21; I have given here the results of using the mordant at three times its usual strength on cellulose fibres.

Cochineal

Coccus cacti are dried insect bodies imported from Mexico and the Canary Islands, where they live on cactus plants. When dried they become hard and resemble metal chips in appearance. They are crushed and placed in muslin and dropped into the dye bath. The depth of colour relates to the amount of cochineal used. Although salt is not needed for dyeing animal fibres, I include it to assist dye penetration in cellulose fibres.

For 100 gm of fibre use:	10 gm of cochineal.
For 1 kg of fibre use:	95 gm of cochineal.
For 1 lb of fibre use:	$1^1/2$ oz of cochineal.

Place the cochineal in the dye bath, and bring it almost to the boil to extract some colour. Allow the bath to cool before entering the wet fibre. Raise the temperature and simmer for 1 hour.

Cochineal on animal fibres

All colours yellow fractionally if acid is added to the bath after dyeing, and colours shift towards purple with the addition of bicarbonate of soda.

Alum	crimson
Chrome	red violet
Copper	burgundy
Iron	dark violet red
Tin	scarlet
No mordant	red purple

Cochineal on silk

Temperature should be kept below simmer.

Alum	burgundy red
Copper	reddish purple
Chrome	brownish purple
Iron	purple
Tin	bluish red

Cochineal on cellulose fibres

Use 10 gm (1 dessertspoon) of salt to 500 gm (1 lb) of fibre. The colours on cellulose fibres are much paler and I recommend giving them a tannic acid bath after mordanting and before dyeing, to give a stronger shade.

		With tannic acid bath
Alum	pale pink	pale lavender
Chrome	pale brown pink	old rose
Copper	pale magenta	brown purple
Iron	pale grey purple	purple grey
Tin	pale coral	bluish coral

Triple mordant without tannic acid or cream of tartar

Alum	pale pink
Chrome	pale magenta
Copper	purple grey
Iron	grey
Tin	coral

Madder

Madder is the root of the *Rubina tinctoria*. We use it in the form of either chips or powder. In an acidic situation it produces vivid oranges and rich browns on wool, medium shades of salmon and rose on silk, and softer paler shades of delicate oranges and salmons on cotton.

For 100 gm of fibre use: 50 gm of madder.
For 1 kg of fibre use: 500 gm of madder.
For 1 lb of fibre use: 8 oz of madder.

Soak the madder overnight in the dye bath. Bring it slowly to simmer point, stirring well during heating. Simmer for 30 minutes. Cool then enter wet fibre and simmer for 1 hour. Allow the fibre to cool in the bath before removing to rinse. The temperature of the dye bath for madder is kept below 82°C (180°F) because heat extracts the stronger brown pigments and the orange and brick red shades disappear. Acid added at the end of dyeing shifts the colours towards yellow, and alkali shifts the colours towards purple.

Madder on animal fibres

Alum	red orange
Chrome	mahogany
Copper	golden brown
Iron	red brown
Tin	vivid orange
No mordant	salmon

Madder on silk

Alum	coral
Copper	light tan
Chrome	pale burgundy
Iron	purple grey
Tin	salmon

Madder on cellulose fibres

		With tannic acid bath
Alum	pale pink	pale coral
Chrome	v. pale blue pink	pale red brown
Iron	v. pale pink	purple grey
Tin	tinted orange	pale salmon
Copper	pale pink brown	pale brown pink

Triple mordant without tannic acid or cream of tartar

Alum	salmon
Chrome	pale mahogany
Copper	pale brown pink
Iron	pale brown grey
Tin	pale orange

Logwood

Logwood is the heartwood of the South American tree *Haematoxylin campeachianum*. It was used for many years, even after synthetic dyes were introduced, for blue and black dyes with chrome and copper mordants. I achieved a strong black on all fibres using a copper mordant. Second and third exhaust dyes gave navy and blue with these mordants, or purples and lavenders using alum or tin mordants. For the paler shades use less logwood than this usual recipe.

For 100 gm of fibre use:	19 gm of logwood.
For 1 kg of fibre use:	187 gm of logwood.
For 1 lb of fibre use:	3 oz of logwood.

Soak the chips overnight wrapped in muslin. Add the liquor and the chips to the dye bath and bring to the boil. Cool the bath then add the wetted fibre. Simmer together for 1 hour.

Logwood on animal fibres

Alum	dark red purple
Copper	black
Chrome	black
Iron	black
Tin	dark purple red
No mordant	red brown

Logwood on silk

Temperature kept below simmer.

Alum	black
Chrome	dark gold brown
Copper	black
Iron	black
Tin	dark burgundy

Logwood on cellulose fibres

		With tannic acid bath
Alum	brown purple	dull purple
Chrome	blue black	black
Copper	medium grey	black
Iron	pale yellow grey	dark grey
Tin	pale buff	dark red purple

Triple mordant without tannic acid or cream of tartar

Alum	smoke purple
Copper	black
Chrome	purple black
Iron	grey
Tin	purple

Brazilwood

Brazilwood is from the heart of the *Caesalpine echinata* tree. The arabic word 'brazil' means bright red. In extract form it was also known as 'sappanwood'. On animal fibres, the colours range from salmon to rust red; they can be yellowed by the addition of acid. Alkali neutralizes the acid in cream of tartar so that colours range from crimson to dark purple. For best results on cellulose fibres, mordant as for animal fibres then give them a tannic acid bath.

For 100 gm of fibre use:	16 gm of brazilwood.
For 1 kg of fibre use:	160 gm of brazilwood.
For 1 lb of fibre use:	2½ oz of brazilwood.

Wrap the brazilwood in muslin and soak it overnight in the water for the dye bath. Enter the wetted fibre and bring this to boiling point before reducing to simmer for 45 minutes.

Brazilwood on animal fibres

The addition of acid to the bath shifts the colours towards yellow. Bicarbonate of soda turns alum to crimson, chrome to blue purple, iron to blue brown, tin to pink and copper to purpley red.

Alum	orange salmon
Chrome	dark purple red
Copper	rusty red
Iron	brown
Tin	pinky salmon
No mordant	pink tan

Brazilwood on silk

Temperature kept below simmer.

Alum	wine red
Copper	dark purple red
Chrome	purple wine
Iron	black
Tin	crimson

Brazilwood on cellulose fibres

		With tannic acid bath
Alum	pale salmon orange	salmon
Chrome	pale blue pink	burgundy
Copper	greyed purple	grey purple
Iron	pale smoky grey	purple grey
Tin	pale orange	red salmon

Triple mordant without tannic acid or cream of tartar

Alum	greyed salmon
Copper	purpled brown
Chrome	purpled salmon
Iron	purpled grey
Tin	pink

Indigo

Indigo is found in the leaves of plants in the form of a colourless glucoside known as indican, which becomes blue when combined with oxygen in the air. To use indican for dyeing the process involves four stages.

1. **Reduction.** Removing the indican from the plant and oxidizing it in water to form white indigo, which is soluble in an alkali.
2. **Solution.** Dissolving the white indigo in some form of alkali in solution, to induce it to attach to the fibres.
3. **Application.** Applying the dissolved white indigo to the fibre in a dye bath. It is still colourless, and because it is also soluble, it will wash away in this form.
4. **Re-oxygenation** of the white indigo on the fibre, in the air, to convert it to an insoluble indigo blue.

Here is a simple diagram to explain the process.

WATER is chemically 2 parts hydrogen and 1 part oxygen, as described in its chemical symbol H_2O.

H_2O —————— Reduce (remove the oxygen)

The free hydrogen combines with oxygen from the indican molecule in the plant, converting it to 'white indigo' which dissolves in alkali.

Apply to fibres in an alkali bath.

Oxidize in atmosphere air. The hydrogen combines with oxygen in the air to form H_2O. Indigo 'white' becomes blue, which is insoluble and therefore very fast.

There is a variety of agents used to reduce oygen, a number of different alkalis, and many different methods for producing an indigo dye.

Agents that reduce oxygen
Bacteria in urine
Iron sulphate
Zinc metal
Sodium hydrosulphite (sodium dithionite)

Alkalis
Potassium hydroxide in ashes
Calcium carbonate in chalk
Quick lime
Slaked lime
Soda ash or washing soda
Ammonia
Caustic soda
Sodium hydroxide which is the strongest alkali and most used.

Older recipes often used ashes or decomposed urea as weak alkalis, and urine containing bacteria as a reducing agent. These weaker solutions took many weeks to react. In some areas plant foliage was mixed with the ashes; in other parts of the world the decomposed foliage was made into balls and stored until required, and the alkali added when dyeing was ready to begin. The smells, often referred to in the recipes, became stronger as the plants broke down whilst steeping. Newer chemicals speed the process. There are many different methods of dyeing with indigo.

Hydrosulphite vat
This recipe I have found satisfactory. The colours from vat dyeing are bright and permanent. They vary in depth of colour depending upon the amount of indigo used, the length of time the wool is left in dye bath, and the number of times the fibre is lifted for airing. Prepare the dye in a very well ventilated room, or better still, dye outdoors. Wear protective clothing and do not inhale the fumes. Keep this dye and all chemical assistants away from children's reach, and away from food. Indigo vats are ruined once the temperature rises above 60°C (140°F). Sodium hydrosulphite has been renamed sodium dithionite.

You will need
85 gm (3 oz) caustic soda
56 gm (2 oz) sodium dithionite / sodium hydrosulphite
56 gm (2 oz) powdered indigo
A large jug of water (temperature approx. 54°C, 130°F)
2 glass jugs each capable of holding 600 ml (1 pint)
An old dye pot
A water thermometer
Glass rods to stir with

To make an indigo stock solution
In a small container grind 56 gm (2 oz) of indigo and add a little warm water to make a liquid paste.

1. Dissolve the caustic soda. Make sure that you do inhale the fumes. Into one of the glass jugs, pour 600 ml (1 pint) of warm water at 54°C (130°F). Very carefully add the caustic soda and stir with a glass rod.
2. Dissolve the sodium hydrosulphite. Into the second glass jug containing 600 ml of water (1 pint), at 54°C (130°F), stir in the hydrosulphite.

Into an old saucepan or bowl stir together the pasted dye, nearly all of the dissolved caustic soda (1) and nearly all of the dissolved hydrosulphite (2).

Warm this to a temperature of 52°C (125°F) and leave it to stand for 30 minutes in a warm place. At the end of this period of time the glass rods, when dipped into the solution, should show a clear yellow liquid. If there are dusty spots of undissolved indigo, add a little of the left-over hydrosulphite solution (2). If the mixture is too thick and milky, add small quantities of caustic soda solution (1) until all is clear yellow.

Dyeing method
1. Fill the dye bath with warm water (50°C, 120°F).
2. Add 56 ml (2 fluid oz) of hydrosulphite solution (2). Stir and leave it to de-oxygenate the water for 20 minutes.
3. Add 28 ml (1 fluid oz) of the indigo stock solution.
4. Keep the bath temperature between 49–54°C (120–130°F). Add the wet fibre and move gently through the dye. Avoid making bubbles throughout the process, and keep the fibre beneath the surface of the liquid. Dye for 30 minutes.
5. Expose the fibre to the air for 30 minutes. The colour will change from yellow to green, and with subsequent redipping, will change from green to blue, pale blue to dark navy. If after several dippings and exposures to air the dye is not as strong as you would have hoped for, increase the amount of stock solution in the dye bath and re-dye.
6. When dyeing is completed, wash the fibre thoroughly in warm detergent water and rinse in clear warm water. Some dyers add one teaspoon of sulphuric acid to the rinse water to enhance the colour. If used, please note that it is highly poisonous and burns the skin. Treat any burns immediately with an alkali solution of bicarbonate of soda.

Indigo sulphuric acid extract
An alternative recipe, which demands the utmost care in preparation, uses sulphuric acid to dissolve the indigo. No airing of fibre and dye is needed.

The advantage of this recipe is that the colours can be regulated to a greater degree, because the indigo-acid extract is quickly absorbed and the colour is completely exhausted in the dye bath. This means that the depth of colour can be controlled by the addition of more indigo acid, or the removal of the fibre once the desired depth is reached. On the adverse side, the dye is less fast to intense sunlight and repeated washings than those from a hydrosulphite vat.

Chalk is added to the mixture to reduce the acidity and to shift the green shades produced in acidic situations to the blues from alkali situations.

To prepare the stock solution, the sulphuric acid needs to be weighed in a glass container. The acid fumes are most powerful, and if you do not have an extractor fan, work outdoors.

Stock solution
28 gm (1 oz) indigo powder
250 gm (8 oz) sulphuric acid in a container
14 gm (1/2 oz) of precipitated chalk

Put the indigo in a glass basin, pour a little acid over it and mix constantly with a glass rod. Add a little chalk. When foaming subsides, add a little more acid and alternate chalk and acid until all are used up. Keep the solution in a glass jar which is tightly stoppered with a material which will not react to the acidic fumes. Glass stoppered bottles are ideal.

Keep the stock solution for one week before using it. Care is required each time the preparation is opened, because the fumes froth and fume as they try to escape. A little water may be added to the solution to reduce the foaming without affecting the dye potential. The solution may be stored indefinitely, but please label it well and store out of reach of children, preferably locked away.

Dyeing method

1. Use 14 ml (^{1}/2 fluid oz) stock solution to 450 gm (1 lb) of unmordanted fibre, and stir it into the dye bath.
2. Heat the water until tepid, then add the wetted fibre.
3. Simmer below boiling for 45 minutes. If the colour is not deep enough, add more of the stock solution.
4. Wash the fibre thoroughly in warm detergent water and rinse well.

Plants containing indican

In previous recipes the indigo is already extracted or prepared ready for dyeing. In areas where indican-bearing plants – *Indigofera suffruticosa, Indigofera tinctoria* and *Isatis tinctoria* (woad) – grow naturally, or have been grown specifically for dyeing, would-be dyers are searching for ways to remove the indican from the plants.

Here in New Zealand the climate is not suitable for *Indigofera,* but many dyers like myself have grown woad with which to experiment. The indican content is minimal, but experiments show that it increases in hot dry climates. The colours are greyed in comparison to indigo powder, but achieving those elusive blues from our own plants gives a great sense of satisfaction.

Here are some recipes that I have tried. They can be used for woad and *Indigofera.*

Recipe 1

1. Shred the leaves and cover them with warm water, leaving an air space in the container. Seal the mixture and keep it in a warm situation for 16–20 days.
2. Add the alkali. Sodium dithionite (hydrosulphite) gives turquoise, ammonia gives dusky blue, and builder's lime gives a strong blue. For 250 gm (8 oz) of fibre add 3 dessertspoons of ammonia, or 1 teaspoon of sodium dithionite or lime.
3. Enter the wetted fibre and move it gently beneath the surface for a few minutes, without making bubbles in the liquid. After 30 minutes expose the fibre to the air for 30 minutes.
4. Repeat the process until the fibre turns from yellow to green, then green to blue. A cold solution may be heated to 49°C (120°F).
5. Leave the final colour exposed to the air overnight.
6. Wash in warm detergent water to which a little vinegar has been added to neutralize any remaining alkali and rinse well.

Recipe 2

A fast method of dyeing involves picking the leaves in late summer, or in a year when the plant does not flower. For my experiments I used one eighth the weight of wool to weight of leaves.

1. Shred the leaves and put them into a glass or stainless steel bowl and pour over boiling water. Allow this to cool to hand hot (49°C, 120°F) then add the alkali. To 250 gm (8 oz) of fibre add 3 dessertspoons of ammonia or 1 teaspoon of sodium dithionite or 1 teaspoon of either baking soda, caustic soda or lime.
2. Enter the wetted fibre and move it gently beneath the surface for a few minutes. Leave for 15 minutes then expose the fibre to the air for 20 minutes. Repeat the process.
3. If the solution becomes cool, it may be heated to 49°C (120°F). For lavender shades heat it a little above this temperature and then you will have the blue shade overdyed with the pink brown colour that is released when the temperature rises and kills the blues.

Recipe 3

This recipe uses the liquid without the leaves.

1. Break up fresh green leaves and cover them with almost boiling water and leave to stand for 5 minutes.
2. Strain off the brownish liquid and add to it a little slaked lime (calcium hydroxide) or ammonia, until it appears greenish. To each litre of liquid add $^{1}/_{4}$ teaspoon of sodium dithionite and keep the liquid warm, though no higher than 49°C (120°F).
3. Slowly enter the wetted fibre and move it gently beneath the surface for a few minutes. Leave for 30 minutes, then expose the fibre to the air for 30 minutes, and repeat the process if necessary.
4. Leave the final colour to air overnight, before washing and rinsing. Add a little vinegar to the wash to neutralize any remaining alkali.

I have received correspondence from dyers who have shredded the leaves, covered them with warm water and completely excluded all air by overflowing the liquid. They kept this for several days in a warm situation. The liquid was drained off and used without any chemical assistants to produce pale blues on wool, by absorption followed by exposure to air.

Other recipes take the liquid strained from the leaves and add alkali as the liquid is beaten or whisked (to introduce the air) until it becomes dark green. This liquor is mixed with equal amounts of stale urine to which half a cup of bran has been added to each litre of urine. Wetted wool is entered and the entire mixture is overflowed to exclude air, and sealed for two weeks. Periods of exposure to air for 30 minutes, followed by redipping into the liquor for 30 minutes, changes the colour through the yellows to greens and blues. The final airing is left overnight. This method of using bran and bacteria in the urine to reduce the oxygen follows the older recipes of extracting blues from plants.

3. USING CHEMICAL DYES

EQUIPMENT

The dye pots and utensils described in Chapter One are also the best for chemical dyeing, though the dye type you are using may cause requirements to vary. Caustic solutions will be mixed in glass or ceramic containers. Plastic containers are very useful when using fibre reactive dyes, but will be unsatisfactory for naphthols. A water thermometer is useful for vat dyes, but is unnecessary when using 'cold' fibre reactives. So before beginning to dye, read the instructions and make a note of the equipment you think you will need. Here is a selection you may find useful:

• Tubs, buckets and baths for dip dyeing.
• Stainless steel or enamelled dye pots and a heat source for 'hot' dyes.
• A water thermometer.
• Glass, stainless steel or fibreglass rods for stirring the dyes.
• Glass or plastic measuring cylinders, beakers or plastic cups.
• A set of accurate scales makes dyeing so much easier, and is essential when using some dyes.
• Best results from many of the dyes require the use of pH testing papers.

When progressing into percentage dyeing, you may find some chemical equipment such as glass beakers, pipettes or eye droppers, and measuring cylinders are a useful addition, and if you are not a confident mathematician a calculator can take the anxiety out of working out dye powder quantities.

Large quantities of rug yarn are suspended over a rod lying across a wash boiler.

HOW TO USE YOUR DYE

If you have a dye and are unsure how to use it, there are two options for you:

1. In the relevant fibre section, find the brand name – ie. Procion, Lanaset – or find the dye class your dye falls into – ie 'acid', 'fibre reactive' or 'basic' – and match it to one of the sections in Chapters Four to Nine. Acid dyes cannot be used for cold pad batching, while fibre reactives can, for instance, so it is important that you should know the class to which your dye belongs.
2. Ask the distributor from whom you purchased the dye to supply you with some instructions on how to use the dye. Some manufacturers are most reluctant to pass on this information, but explain to them that you are not asking for any secret recipe!

READING DYE LABELS

The label on the dye should give you information not only about the dye class but also about the colour that you might expect from the dye. For example, one of my dyes has a label, 'Lanasol Violet 3B'. From the trade name I know that it is a fibre reactive dye and I can match the trade name to the relevant dye recipes. The hue or colour is violet, and the '3B' tells me that it is quite blueish.

Suffix meanings: R, B, G
Since the major chemical companies originated in the German speaking areas of Europe, many suffixes, including those relating to colour direction, are in the Germanic form.

R = Rot = Red. B = Blau = Blue. G = Gelb = Yellow.

If the dye is labelled 'Red B', the suffix 'B' indicates that while the colour or hue is red, it has a leaning towards blue.
These are the positions that they might assume on the colour wheel.

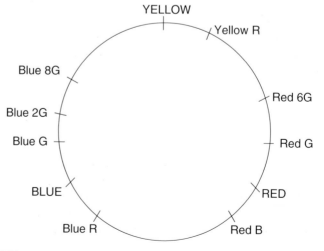

The number accompanying the suffix indicates a greater or lesser degree of movement around the colour wheel. Red 4B is therefore much more purple than Red B, in fact a rather royal shade of red. For a more complete discussion of colour see Chapter Thirteen. Here are some commonly used dyes:

Red B: a blue red, crimson   Blue 8G: turquoise
Red 4B: a purple red   Blue R: towards red, ultramarine
Red G: scarlet   Yellow G: bright sunshine yellow
Red 6G: a yellower red   Yellow R: a dull brownish yellow, ochre
Blue G: a sky blue, cobalt

Other suffixes   S = soluble, *or*
L = Lightfast   S = made for silk
Conc = Concentrated   P = suitable for printing, *or*
N = New dye   P = fast to perspiration
Nyl = Especially for Nylon
KWS = cold water soluble

Concentration of dye powders

Some dyes also have a number that indicates how concentrated the dye powders are. Unless otherwise stated, dyes are assumed to be 100% a dye. With increasing freight costs, it makes sense to produce a more concentrated dye. When dyes that previously had no concentration number suddenly appear on the market with '200', or '200%' after the suffix, you are alerted to the fact that they are now twice as strong and you will only need half the previous amount of dye to achieve the same depth of dye colour. Conversely, I am no longer able to purchase a red brown dye labelled '200' from my usual supplier, and because my new dye stock has been reduced to 100% by the distributor I need to recalculate the amount of dye to use in my usual recipe.

HOW MUCH DYE TO USE

Once you have chosen your basic colour (hue), ie Red B, a further decision is required: how pale or dark do you require the colour to be? This is referred to as colour **value** or **depth of shade**. Some books refer to 'depth of dye', which is just the same. A dark depth of shade will require proportionately more dye powder than a pale depth of shade. Chapter Thirteen explains how to prepare value cards for a visual reference to different depths of shade.

The informal approach

Here is a useful rule of thumb to how much dye powder to use to dye 450 gm (1 lb) of fibre:

To a pale depth of shade: $^1/2$ tsp dye (roughly 2.5 gm)
To a light/medium depth of shade: 1 tsp dye (roughly 5 gm)
To a medium/dark depth of shade: 2 tsp dye (roughly 10 gm)
To a dark depth of shade: 3 tsp dye (roughly 15 gm)
To a very dark depth of shade: 4 tsp dye (roughly 20 gm)

The amount of dye used is always in ratio to the weight of fibre to be dyed. If the weight of fibre increases, the weight of dye increases simultaneously to achieve the same dye shade. Stage one is therefore always **weigh the fibre**.

This works reasonably well until you wish to dye a similar shade again, and you start to question: 'Did I use level or heaped teaspoons?'

Another approach is to mix 2 level tablespoons of dye to 1 litre (1 quart) of water to make a dye solution which is easier to measure. Pour a little at a time into the dye pot, but be careful because if you add too much you cannot get it out again. Keep a few records of how many millilitres or teaspoons you have used. Mix them like paints and test the colours to see if they are what you wanted. If you put them into a glass container and hold it to daylight, you will get a good idea of the colour, but not the depth.

For many years I managed very well with this method, but I was unable to repeat a colour exactly and therefore dyed more yarn than I needed, so wasting dye and fibre.

PERCENTAGE DYEING

To be able to repeat or match a dye colour, it is necessary to measure accurately, always using the same method. Percentage dyeing enables you to do this, and is really easy to work out if you take it step by step.

Let us write depth of shade as a percentage.

Very pale shades:	$\frac{1}{16}$%	(0.062%) =	0.062 gm of dye to 100 gm fibre
Pale shades:	$\frac{1}{8}$%	(0.125%) =	0.125 gm of dye to 100 gm fibre
Light shades:	$\frac{1}{4}$%	(0.25%) =	0.25 gm of dye to 100 gm fibre
Light/medium:	$\frac{1}{2}$%	(0.5%) =	0.5 gm of dye to 100 gm fibre
Medium shades:	1%	(1.0%) =	1.0 gm of dye to 100 gm fibre
Medium/dark:	2%	(2.0%) =	2.0 gm of dye to 100 gm fibre
Dark shades:	4%	(4.0%) =	4.0 gm of dye to 100 gm fibre

Double weave jacket using fibre reactive and acid dyes.
Dyed, woven and tailored by Elizabeth Sproull.

Hand woven fabrics with handspun weft yarns, dyed in the fleece with fibre reactive dyes. Elizabeth spinning wheel by Ashford in the foreground. Dyed, spun and woven by Ann Milner.

Pasting a dye powder. Put the dye powder into a cup or beaker, add two drops of liquid detergent or wetting agent, then enough cold water to mix to a thin paste. Add hot but not boiling water and stir rapidly until all is dissolved. The dye may be stored or used immediately for dyeing.

Note that wool does not absorb much more than 4% of its own weight.

Using a formula

Here is a simple formula to calculate how much dye powder to use:

weight of fibre x depth of shade (%) = weight of dye powder

100 gm of fibre at 1% depth of shade =	100 x 1% =	1 gm of dye
400 gm of fibre at 2% depth of shade =	400 x 2% =	8 gm of dye
200 gm of fibre at ¼% depth of shade =	200 x 0.25% =	0.5 gm of dye

If you are more comfortable using fractions you could do it this way:

$$\frac{\text{weight of fibre x depth of shade}}{100}$$

100 gm fibre at 1% depth of shade = $\dfrac{100 \times 1}{100}$ = 1 gm of dye

400 gm fibre at 2% depth of shade = $\dfrac{400 \times 2}{100}$ = 8 gm of dye

200 gm fibre at ¼% depth of shade =

$\dfrac{200 \times \frac{1}{4}}{100}$ = $\dfrac{200 \times 1}{100 \times 4}$ = $\dfrac{200}{400}$ = ¹/₂ (0.5) gm dye

PERCENTAGE STOCK SOLUTIONS

When dyeing very small amounts of fibre, the weight of dyestuff and dye powder becomes too difficult to measure accurately and a dye solution is easier to use. I usually make a 1% solution using 1 gm of dye to every 100 ml of water.

To make a 1% dye solution

Weigh 10 gm of dye powder (approximately 2 tsp). Put the dye into a litre container and add two drops of liquid detergent or wetting agent, and sufficient **cold** water to mix a thin paste. Crush all lumps of dye. Add 500 ml (2 cups) of hot, but not boiling water and mix thoroughly for two minutes until all dye is dissolved. Make this up to 1 litre with cold water. Make sure that there is no dye still undissolved at the bottom of the spoon or container, or the dye will no longer be a 1% solution.

Pour the dye into a bottle with a stopper. Label it with the name of the dye, the colour and coding, then the strength of the solution. For safety, do not use soft drink bottles and store away from the reach of young children. If the dye settles or curdles during storage, warm the liquid until the dye re-dissolves.

Small amounts of **1%** dye may be made using, for example:

5 gm of dye powder made up to 500 ml in volume
1 gm of dye powder made up to 100 ml in volume
0.5 gm of dye powder made up to 50 ml in volume

To make weaker solutions

When dyeing small amounts of fibre to a pale shade, the 1% solution is too strong. A solution one tenth of the strength of a 1% solution (**0.1%** strength of dye) has 1 gm of dye to 1000 ml or 0.1 gm to 100 ml of solution. You can make it a more accurate measurement by preparing it from the already mixed 1% solution:

100 ml of 1% solution + 900 ml water makes 1 litre of 0.1% dye
30 ml of 1% solution + 270 ml water makes 300 ml of 0.1% dye
10 ml of 1% solution + 90 ml water makes 100 ml of 0.1% dye

A **0.01%** solution, which is 10 times weaker again, or one hundredth the strength of a 1% solution, has 1 gm of dye to 10,000 ml of solution.

10 ml of 1% solution + 990 ml water makes 1 litre of 0.01% dye
3 ml of 1% solution + 297 ml water makes 300 ml of 0.01% dye
1 ml of 1% solution + 99 ml water makes 100 ml of 0.01% dye

To make a very weak **0.001%** solution (1 gm in 100,000 ml):

1 ml of 1% solution + 999 ml water
or 10 ml of 0.1% solution + 990 ml water
or 100 ml of 0.01% solution + 900 ml water
makes 1 litre 0.001% dye

To dye 1 kilo (1000 gm)		To dye 100 gm		To dye 1 gm	
Depth of Shade	*Dye*	*Depth of Shade*	*Dye*	*Depth of Shade*	*Dye*
2%	20 gm powder	2%	200 ml of 1% solution	2%	20 ml of 0.1% solution
1%	10 gm powder	1%	100 ml of 1% solution	1%	10 ml of 0.1% solution
½ %	5 gm powder	½ %	50 ml of 1% solution	½ %	5 ml of 0.1% solution
¼ %	2.5 gm powder	¼ %	25 ml of 1% solution	¼ %	25 ml of 0.01% solution
⅛ %	1.25 gm powder	⅛ %	12.5 ml of 1% solution	⅛ %	12.5 ml of 0.01% solution
¹⁄₁₆ %	0.625 gm powder	¹⁄₁₆ %	6.25 ml of 1% solution	¹⁄₁₆ %	6.25 ml of 0.01% solution
¹⁄₃₂ %	0.3125 gm powder	¹⁄₃₂ %	3.12 ml of 1% solution	¹⁄₃₂ %	3.12 ml of 0.01% solution

Above is a simplified table showing how much dye solution or powder to use for 1 kilo (1000 gm), 100 gm and 1 gm of fibre. Multiply the dye quantity as applicable for your fibre weight (ie, for 300 gm multiply dye required for 100 gm by 3).

The amount of dye to be used may also be calculated mathematically.

Calculating how much solution to use
Weigh the fibre to be dyed, then keep two distinct ideas in your head. One percentage will be depth of shade required (how dark). The other percentage will be the strength of the dye solution used (how weak). For the mathematically insecure, a calculator will make the calculations simple (and accurate).

The formula is:

$$\frac{\text{weight of fibre (gms) x depth of shade (\%)}}{\text{strength of dye solution (\%)}} = \text{volume of dye solution (mls)}$$

You could remember it as:

$$\frac{\text{W (weight) x D (depth of shade)}}{\text{S (strength of solution)}} = \text{V (volume of dye solution)}$$

Here are some examples.

• To dye 5 gm of fibre to a pale ¼% (0.25%) depth of shade using a 0.1% dye solution:

$$\frac{\text{W x D}}{\text{S}} = \frac{5 \times 0.25}{0.1} = 12.5 \text{ ml of 0.1\% dye solution}$$

• To dye 5 gm of fibre to a dark 3% depth of dye using a 1% dye solution:

$$\frac{\text{W x D}}{\text{S}} = \frac{5 \times 3}{1} = 15 \text{ ml of 1\% dye solution}$$

This formula holds true for estimating the amount of undiluted dye (100% strength) to use for larger amounts of fibre (refer back to p. 55). For example, to dye 500 gm of fibre to a medium/light depth of 2%:

$$\frac{W \times D}{S} = \frac{500 \times 2}{100} = 10 \text{ gm dye powder}$$

Reducing the additives to solutions
When dyeing small amounts of fibre, the necessary additives will also need to be measured in very small amounts, which can be difficult. Reducing the additives to a percentage solution as well helps to ensure accuracy.

If a recipe states 'use 4 gm of ammonium sulphate to 100 gm of fibre', this is the same as saying 'use 4% ammonium sulphate to weight of fibre'. Mix 4gm with warm water to make up to 100 ml in volume. You now have a 4% solution. Use 1 ml of this solution to each 1 gm of fibre.

Glauber's salt is used with some dyes when dyeing pale shades, at a rate of 10%. Mix 10 gm of the salt and make up to 100 ml with warm water and you now have a 10% solution. Use 1 ml for each 1 gm of fibre.

Levellers such as Albegal B are used in some cases at 1%. This can be mixed by measuring 1 ml and adding 99 ml of water to make it up to 100 ml of 1% solution. Use 1 ml to each 1 gm of fibre. For 1.5% addition measure 1.5 ml and 98.5 ml of water to make it up to 100 ml of 1.5% solution. Use 1 ml to each 1 gm of fibre.

DYE APPLICATION

The manner in which the dyes are used will depend upon the project you have planned. The principles are the same for all different fibres, but remember protein fibres require an acidic environment and cellulose fibres require an alkaline environment. The additives, therefore, will vary, according to your fibre and dye type. Refer to the following chapters for instructions and recipes for your dye, fibre and the appropriate technique.

Preparation of fibres for dyeing
Protein fibres must be clean and free from lanolin and dirt which will prevent successful dyeing, and cellulose fibres must be free of starch size, waxes and pectins which will react with the dye. Scouring instructions may be found in Chapter One.

Care in handling
Rubber gloves and a good apron or overalls are essential. Wearing a face mask when handling dye powders or caustic materials is sensible and, of course, all chemicals must be well labelled and kept out of reach of children.

Measurements
Note that in recipes where imperial and metric measures are given they may not be exactly equivalent. Use *either* metric *or* imperial measurements, not a mixture! A table of measurements may be found on p. 172.

4. CHEMICAL DYE BATHS FOR PROTEIN FIBRES

Protein fibres include all animal fibres, and the same dyes can be used successfully on silk (taking care not to increase the heat beyond 84°C, 185°F) and nylon.

DYE BATH DYEING

Dye bath dyeing for protein fibres is often referred to as **exhaust dyeing**, since the dye reacts with fibre, water and additives until it is fully taken up or 'exhausted'. At this stage the dye liquor should be clear.

The secret to successful dye bath dyeing, whether natural or chemical, is the same. The temperature of the dye bath is increased very slowly, whilst the fibre is rotated frequently. As boiling point approaches, the rotating ceases. The recommended additives are all present in the dye bath, and the fibre is wet and well scoured when it is put into the bath.

Additives for hot exhaust dyeing include acid and levelling or wetting agents.

Levels of acidity and alkalinity

All dyes for protein fibres need an acidic dye bath. The level of acidity is measured on a pH scale.

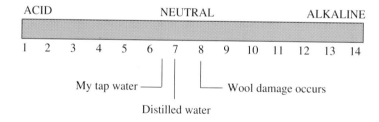

To measure the pH of your dye bath accurately, you will need to purchase some pH testing paper, similar to litmus paper. I buy mine from a chemical supplier to the medical profession. For wool dyeing I choose a range from pH 3 to pH 7. Test the pH of the dye bath with all of the additives except the dye, which will colour the paper and prevent a reading.

Acetic acid is usually used to make the dye bath acidic. Vinegar is approximately 4% acetic acid but when used for large volumes of fibres it becomes an expensive additive. Acetic acid may be purchased from a chemist or from photography suppliers. It comes in several strengths, but $33\frac{1}{3}$% is the preferred strength for safety, especially if you are working with a group. More experienced dyers may prefer to use glacial acetic acid at 80–90%. This is corrosive to the skin and to metal, and damages the mucus membranes if inhaled. It may be weakened to $33\frac{1}{3}$% by diluting it with water. Always **add acid to water** or the fumes will be forced upward out of the container or dye bath, and into the face of the mixer.

Levellers or wetting agents

These coat the fibre causing the dye molecule to move around the fibre looking for a dye site, preventing immediate, patchy or 'unlevel' dyeing.

Levellers are chemically similar to liquid detergents and therefore if you are not certain which to use, or you haven't the correct leveller for your dye, substitute liquid dish wash detergent. However, each dye has an accompanying leveller designed specifically for it, and this will give slightly better results than the liquid detergent alternative.

Never use a leveller designed for a different dye. I once ruined several kilos of rug yarn by adding the wrong leveller, which stuck to the dye and merely coated the fibre and the dye bath.

Most levellers are added at a rate of 1% weight of fibre (1 ml to each 100 gm or 5 ml (1 tsp) to 500 gm (approx 1 lb) of fibre).

Unlevel dyes are produced by:

1. Bringing the dye bath to boiling point too quickly;
2. Greasy yarn or fibre;
3. No levelling agent, or using too much levelling agent;
4. Insufficient turning of the fibre while dyeing.

General notes
- Fibre appears a darker shade when wet.
- Individual dyes take at different temperatures, so do not be alarmed if your mixed colour seems to have left one hue in the dye bath, when another has fixed to the fibre. Continue dyeing for the stated period of time to allow all dyes to fix.
- Use the correct leveller for the dye. If in doubt, substitute a neutral liquid detergent.
- If the colour appears satisfactory part-way through the dyeing process and there is still dye in the bath, the fibre may be removed, but the dye still needs to be fixed. Place the fibre into another warm bath to which acetic acid has been added to give the correct pH level. Bring this to boiling or simmer point, over the recommended period of time.
- Safety is always important when handling dyes, especially when dyeing in a home or kitchen environment.
- Add acid *to* water and not the other way around, to avoid rising fumes.
- Neutralize all dye baths before pouring them down the drain. Use household ammonia to neutralize acid baths and test that the pH is 6.5–7. Some city water supplies are slightly acidic.
- Do not be overwhelmed by charts and percentages. Some excellent results come from 'nearly correct' dyeing.
- Experimentation leads to creation!

Liquor ratio

Remember the liquor ratio (L/R) is the amount of water used in the dye bath in proportion to the weight of fibre to be dyed. Refer to p.16 for a more detailed description.

DYE TYPES SUITABLE FOR PROTEIN FABRICS

Find the major category into which your dye fits, and you will find it will react in the manner described. The trade name of the dye is not so important.

Fibre reactive dyes

Fibre reactive dyes form an excellent chemical bond between fibre and dye. They are exceedingly washfast and lightfast when used with the hot exhaust method, providing that adequate boiling time has been maintained and the correct acidity level achieved. They are therefore suitable for any fibre that needs frequent washing, and ideal for felt dyeing. Commercially they are used for machine washable fabrics.

Brand name	Manufacturer	Page reference
Cibacrolan	Ciba Geigy	65
Drimalan F	Sandoz	66
Hostalan	Hoechst	65
Lanasol	Ciba Geigy	64
Procilan	ICI	–
Verofix	Bayer	–

Cold fibre reactive dyes such as Procion MX, Panfix W or Earth Palette dyes do not require heat because the dyes fix at a warm room temperature over a period of time. This makes them suitable for dip-dyeing or for direct application methods (see pp. 95–103), but they can also be used in a 'cold' dye bath.

Brand name	Manufacturer	Page reference
Procion MX	ICI	67
Panfix W		68
Earth Palette		68

Lanaset dyes

These are a mixture of two parts fibre reactive Lanasol dye and one part Irgalan premetallized 1:2 dye. They are suitable for all animal fibres. Silk dyes well, but will be slightly lighter than wool in the same dye bath. Nylon also dyes well, but the pH level will need to be around 6.5 to avoid fibre damage. See p. 68.

Acid dyes

Acid dyes were developed for use on animal fibres. They all need acid in the dye bath to assist the chemical bond between fibre and dye, water and heat.

There are three main classes:

• **Acid levelling:** These dyes are noted for giving good level dyeing throughout the fibre. They produce strong, bright hues which mix well together to give a wide range of colours. Their moderate washfastness can be helped by keeping subsequent washing temperatures below 40°C (105°F).

The dyes are suitable for all animal fibres, including silk, which will be a lighter shade than wool in the same dye bath. See p. 69.

Brand name	Manufacturer
Amacid	American Colour Chemical
Erio	Ciba-Geigy
Intracid	Compton and Knowles
Kiton	Ciba-Geigy
Lissamine	ICI
Sandolan E	Sandoz
Suprecen	Bayer

• **Acid milling:** These dyes are less level than the acid levelling dyes. The colour range of the dyes is limited, but the colours are bright. See p. 70.

Brand name	Manufacturer:
Coomassie	ICI
Eriosin (silk)	Ciba-Geigy
Polar (wool)	Ciba-Geigy
Sandolan N	Sandoz
Supranol	Bayer

• **Supermilling or fast acid:** These dyes contain a selection of bright colours, but do not readily produce a level dye. Glauber's salt should *not* be used with this dye because it speeds up the take of the dye, giving patchy results. See p. 70.

Brand name	Manufacturer
Carbolan	ICI
Irganol	Ciba-Geigy
Any dye named 'brilliant'	

See also **Sandolan MF dyes** (p. 73).

Pre-metallized dyes

These are so named because they combine metal atoms with dye molecules. The colours are not so brilliant as acid levelling dyes. They are divided into two groups.

• **1:1 Premetallized dyes** (1 metal atom to 1 dye molecule): These dyes require a very strong acid dye bath and are not used by the home dyer.

Brand name	Manufacturer
Neolan	Ciba Geigy
Palatine	BASF

• **1:2 Premetallized dyes** (1 metal atom to 2 dye molecules): If silk and wool are placed in the same dye bath the colour should be the same on both fibres. The dyes are washfast and lightfast, which makes them good for felt. They are dull compared with some dyes but may be mixed with supermilling dyes (i.e.

Irganol) to achieve brighter shades, because both require the same dye bath. See p. 73.

Brand name	Manufacturer
Cibalan	Ciba-Geigy
Intralan	Compton Knowles
Irgalan ('Panhue')	Ciba-Geigy
Isolan	Bayer
Lanasyn	Sandoz
Lanasan CF	Sandoz

Basic dyes

Basic dyes are the earliest class of synthetic dye, and are suitable for animal fibres, including silk. Although the colours are brilliant, the lightfast and washfast qualities are very poor and the fabric needs to be dry cleaned. See p. 74.

Brand name
Tinfix
Sennelier

Direct dyes

These are very similar to the acid levelling dyes, but are really designed for use on cellulose fibres. When using these dyes to dye silk, wool or any other animal fibres, salt is omitted from the dye bath and acetic acid or white vinegar is substituted. If these dyes are used for silk, steaming will be required to heat fix the dyes. For further information see p. 86.

All purpose, household or union dyes.

Each dye, eg Rit, is a mixture of dyes suitable for protein and cellulose fibres. Chapter Five has more details about these dyes. If salt is recommended by the manufacturer, it may be omitted for protein fibres.

Vat dyes

Vat dyes will dye animal fibres, but the concentration of alkali needs to be weaker than for cellulose dyeing to avoid damage to the fibres. The recipe for natural indigo on pp. 45–46 is suited to protein fibres, and the recipe may also be used with any of the synthetic vat dyes. For further information see p. 89.

Napthol dyes

Napthol or azoic dyes are more usually used on cellulose fibres but may be used on protein fibres. For further information see p. 91.

FIBRE REACTIVE DYES

Fibre reactive dyes require an acidic dye bath for dyeing animal fibres. The amount of acid used relates to the amount of dye used (a darker dye needs more acid), and pH-testing papers are very useful. Ammonium sulphate is often used to release acid slowly during dyeing.

Levelling agents are used, and each chemical company has its own brand name of leveller to complement its dye. They are non-toxic and are related to liquid detergents, which may be substituted if necessary. Too great a volume of leveller prevents a good take-up of dye.

The dye recipes indicate a slow temperature rise over a given period of time to promote even dyeing. Levelling takes place below 85°C, 185°F, and the fibre is gently rotated during this period. Once above this temperature, the reaction takes place and levelling ceases.

Fibre reactives may be used in conjunction with other dye classes providing the additives for fibre reactives are used, and that the necessary acid level has been reached.

LANASOL

L/R: 30:1　　　　　　　　　　　　　　**Washfast quality:** excellent.
pH level: 4.5 strong – 6.5 pale shades　　**Lightfast quality:** excellent.

Dye bath additives: Albegal B as levelling agent.
Ammonium sulphate releases acid during dyeing. Use 4 gm to each 100 gm of fibre (4%).
Acetic acid to enable the reaction to take place.
Glauber's salt retards dyeing. It is useful for pastel shades but may be omitted for medium and strong shades.

Lanasol has bright colours, but subdued colours previously obtained by natural dyeing may also be achieved using the trichromatic dyes Yellow 4G, Rd 6G, and Blue 3G. Thesehave a similar rate of take-up and are therefore most compatible.

LANASOL Additives for shade required (mls per 100 gm fibre)	Very pale	Pale	Light	Light/Med.	Medium	Med./Dark	Dark
Dye powder %	0.25	0.5	1	1.5	2	3	4
pH level	6.5	6.5	6–6.5	5.6–6	5.3–5.6	5.1–5.3	4.5–5.1
Amm. sulphate %	4	4	4	4	4	4	4
Albegal B %	1	1	1	1	1	1.5	2
Glauber's salt %	10	10	5	–	–	–	–
Acetic acid (33) %	1	1	1.6	2	3	4	4.5
(80%) %	0.5	0.5	0.5	1	1.5	2	2–4

Dyeing method

1. Heat the dye bath to 50°C (120°F). This is hand-hot. Add the acetic acid, then the Albegal B.
2. Enter clean and wetted fibre and leave it to soak for 10 minutes. Measure the pH and adjust if necessary.
3. Remove the fibre or push it to the side and add the dye in solution. Stir well and re-enter the fibre.
4. Over 45 minutes raise the temperature to 85°C (184°F) whilst rotating the fibre regularly.
5. Raise the temperature to boiling and then maintain simmer point for 30 minutes without touching the fibre.
6. Allow the fibre to cool in the liquid, which should be exhausted of all dye. If not, you may need a little more acid, or the fibre may have accepted all the dye possible. I have found it advisable to leave all strong dyes to cool completely in the dye bath, and note that more dye has been taken up during this time. When cool, wash and rinse the fibre well.

CIBRACROLAN

Use in the same manner as Lanasol dyes, but double the amount of acetic acid. In New Zealand, some dyes packaged under the label 'Lanasol Blue 8G' have been Cibacrolan dyes.

HOSTALAN DYES

L/R: 30:1   **Washfast qualities:** excellent
pH level: 4.7–5.5   **Lightfast qualities:** excellent

Dye bath additives: Remol GES as levelling agent.
Ammonium sulphate: 2 gm to 100 gm of fibre (2%).
Acetic acid.

HOSTALAN Additives for shade required (mls per 100 gm fibre)	**Pale**	**Light**	**Medium**	**Dark**
Dye powder %	1	2	3	4
pH level	5.5	5.2	5	4.7
Amm. sulphate %	2	2	2	2
Remol GES %	1.5	1.5	1.5	–
Hostalan K %	–	5	5	5
Dye time at boiling (mins)	20–45	60	70	90

Note
•Remol GES has a defoaming agent. Remol GE may also be used.
• Glauber's salt is never used with this dye.

Hostalan dyes require hot water to dissolve them thoroughly. Paste the dye powder with a little cold water, then add hot water, up to 20 times the quantity. Increase the temperature to 80°C (176°F), stirring really well for two minutes. It is then ready to add to the dye bath.

Dyeing method
1. Prepare the dye bath with hand-hot water, 45°C (108°F).
2. Add ammonium sulphate, leveller Remol GES and acetic acid.
3. Enter the clean wetted fibre and allow it to soak for 10 minutes.
4. Test the pH and adjust if necessary. Remove the fibre or push it to one side, and add the dye. Stir well and re-enter the fibre.
5. Over a period of 40 minutes, raise the temperature to 80°C (176°F) and rotate the fibre regularly. For pale to medium shades allow the fibre to rest at this temperature for 25 minutes, then bring to the boil. For darker shades, omit this resting period, and go straight to boil.
6. Bring to the boil and maintain this temperature for a fast dye. Dark shades may need more acid at this stage.
7. When the dye bath has cooled a little, it may be neutralized with Hostalan salt K to remove all unreacted dye molecules, and to make the dye liquid safe to drain away. Use 5 gm of Hostalen K to each 100 gm of fibre.

Hostalan also has trichromatic colours with a similar dye take-up, making them most compatible. They are: Brilliant Yellow E–G, Red E–G, and Blue E–FB.

DRIMALAN F

L/R: 30:1   **Washfast quality:** good
pH level: 4.0–6.0   **Lightfast quality:** good

Dye bath additives: Lyogen FN liquid as levelling agent.
Acetic acid to assist the dye.
Glauber's salt to retard the dye on paler shades.

Drimalan F has brilliant shades, especially in the red and yellow range.

DRIMALAN F Additives for shade required. (mls per 100 gm fibre)	Pale	Medium	Med./Dark
Dye powder %	1	2	3–4
pH level	5–6	4.5–5	4–4.5
Lyogen FN	1	1	2–4
Glauber's salt %	10	5	–
Acetic acid (80%) %	1.5	1.5–2	2–4

Dyeing method

1. Prepare the dye bath (40°C, 104°F), add acetic acid and Glauber's salt for pale shades, then add leveller.
2. Enter clean wetted fibre, and allow it to soak for 10 minutes.
3. Remove the fibre or push it to one side. Check the pH level and adjust if necessary, then add the dye in solution.
4. Over 20 mins raise the temperature to 65°C (140°F) and hold it for 20 mins.
5. Raise the temperature over 30 mins to 98°C (208°F) and simmer: pale shades for 20 mins, medium shades for 30 mins, and dark shades for 60 mins.
6. Cool the fibre in the dye bath before removing it to wash and rinse well.

'COLD' FIBRE REACTIVE DYES

PROCION MX

Washfast quality: Good   **Lightfast quality:** Good

Dye bath additives: Urea to swell the fibre and to act as a solubilizing agent.
Acetic acid to enable dye fixation.
Teric as levelling agent.
Sodium bisulphite increases dye take-up.

Procion MX is a 'cold' fibre reactive dye that was basically designed for cellulose fibres, but may be used for animal fibres, silk and nylon with the addition of sodium bisulphite, which can be purchased from dye distributers. This is extremely reactive with the dye and is therefore added just before the dyes are used. The amount of sodium bisulphite increases with the amount of dye used. Dyes sold under the trade name Dylon contain such a high proportion of Procion MX that they may be used in the same manner.

The recipe below makes 1 litre of dye solution using 10 gm (2 tsp) of dye. You may increase or decrease the amount of dye, depending on the shade required, and you may blend dye colours together.

Dyeing method

1. Pour 500 ml (2 cups) of boiling water over 300 gm of urea. Stir until dissolved. Heat the water again if necessary to dissolve it all.
2. Paste the dye in a beaker with a little cold water. Add this to the urea solution. Ten gm of dye gives a medium shade.
3. Add 10 ml (2 tsp) of Teric, and 5 ml of acetic acid 30 % strength.
4. Add sufficient cold water to make the solution up to 1 litre. Test the dye colour on a sample to see if it is what you wanted. It will be lighter when dry.
5. Just before dyeing begins, add the sodium bisulphite. Use 10 gm (2 tsp) for light to medium shades, 15 gm (3 tsp) for medium shades, and 20 gm (4 tsp) for strong shades.
6. Enter the scoured, **dry** fibre, yarn, or fabric. Submerge it and gently squeeze it to work the dye into all parts of the fibre. Leave the fibre to soak for 20 mins.
7. Batch age (see p. 102) for 24 hours or, on cold days, for 48 hours.

To make smaller amounts of dye in several colours for dip-dyeing, mix a solution of urea, leveller, sodium bisulphite and acetic acid as before. Arrange small containers ready for the dye, and paste dye powder in each with a little cold water. Stirring thoroughly, add the urea solution and make it up to the desired amount. The reaction of these dyes wears off after one and a half hours, so you will need to work quickly.

PANFIX W

This dye is used in the same manner as the Procion MX except that 3 gm (1 tsp) of citric acid is used instead of the acetic acid, and 2 ml Scourbrite leveller replaces the 10 ml of Teric.

The advantage of this dye is its speed of fixation. It has a very fast reaction time of 6–12 hours when batch aged in polythene at room temperature. This time may be reduced by placing the dyed fibre in a plastic oven bag or foil, and baking it in an oven temperature 80°C (176°F) for 15 minutes.

EARTH PALETTE DYES

These cold water fibre reactive dyes have all of the necessary chemicals already incorporated into the dye. Simply stir them into a volume of hot water. They have excellent wash- and lightfast qualities.

Fixing agent A may be added when dyeing greasy unscoured fibres, so that some grease may be retained in the fibre if required.

The dye is in solution and therefore percentages are easily worked out. The amount of dye suggested for medium depth of dye is 100–150 ml of dye to 100 gm of fibre. The dye liquid should be clear when the dye is exhausted.

The fibre is batch aged for 24 hours at room temperature of 20–25°C (68–75°F). If the dye has not fully taken, leave it to age for another 24 hours, perhaps in a warmer place such as the airing cupboard. Faster fixation may be achieved by placing the fibre in an oven bag and baking it at 100°C (212°F) for 10–15 minutes.

FIBRE REACTIVE/PREMETALLIZED 1:2 DYES

LANASET

L/R: 30:1   **Washfast quality:** good
pH level: 4.5–5.0   **Lightfast quality:** good

Dye bath additives: Albegal SET as levelling agent
Acetic acid to give the correct pH level.
Glauber's salt to retard the dyeing of paler shades.

The dyes are available in a wide range of bright colours, but subtle colours are also possible.

Before adding the dye powder to the bath, mix it with a little cold water to make a thin paste, then add very warm water (76°C, 170°F) and stir well for two minutes.

LANASET Additives for shade required. (mls per 100 gm fibre)	Pale	Light	Medium	Dark
Dye powder %	0.5	1	2	4
pH level	5	5	4.5	4.5
Albegal SET %	1	1	1	1
Glauber's salt %	10	5	–	–
Acetic acid (56%) %	1	1.5	2	4

Dyeing method
1. Prepare dye bath with warm water 48°C (120°F) and add the acetic acid, Glauber's salt for pale shades, then the leveller.
2. Enter the clean wetted fibre and leave it to soak for 10 minutes.
3. Remove the fibre or push it to one side, test the pH and adjust if necessary, then add the dye in solution. Stir.
4. Over a period of 45 minutes, raise the temperature to just below boiling point. (For silk the upper limit is 84°C, 185°F.)
5. Maintain this temperature for 15 minutes for pale shades, 40 minutes for dark shades.
6. Cool the dye bath before removing the fibre to wash and rinse it.

ACID DYES

ACID LEVELLING DYES

L/R: 30:1   **Washfast quality:** moderate
pH level: 3–4   **Lightfast quality:** moderate/good

Dye bath additives: Acetic acid to assist dye bond.
                 Glauber's salt (sodium sulphate) to retard dye take up.

Dyeing method
1. Weigh the dry fibre to assess how much dye to use (refer pp51–57), then wet the clean fibre for dyeing.
2. Heat the dye bath to 30°C (86°F). Add 10% Glauber's salt for pale shades, 5% for light shades, and omit for medium and dark shades.
3. Add the dye and stir well.

4. Enter the wetted fibre and slowly increase the temperature to 82°C, 180°F.
5. Remove the fibre from the bath or push it to one side whilst adding the acetic acid.

For

28% strength acid:	10% (10 ml to each 100 g of fibre)
33 % strength acid:	9% (9 ml to each 100 g of fibre)
96 % strength acid:	3% (3 ml to each 100 g of fibre)

Stir well and replace the fibre.
6. Slowly increase the temperature to boiling and hold this for 30 minutes to fix the dyes. (Silk highest temperature 84°C, 185°F.)
7. Allow the fibre to cool in the dye bath before washing in a neutral detergent and rinsing well.

ACID MILLING DYES

L/R: 30:1   **Washfast quality:** good
pH level: 5.2–6.2 (weak acid)   **Lightfast quality:** good

Dye bath additives: 10% ammonium sulphate to release acid slowly into the bath. Use 4 gm for each 100 gm of fibre (4%). (Ammonium sulphate is a fertilizer readily available in garden shops.)

Dyeing method
This recipe is the same as that for acid levelling dyes, except the additives change. When the dye bath becomes warm at 30°C (86°F), add the ammonium sulphate and the dye and stir well. Enter the wetted fibre and raise the temperature to boiling point and retain it for 45 minutes.

Some dyers prefer to omit the ammonium sulphate and use acetic acid instead, to bring the pH level to 5.2–6.2. Add this *either* before the dye, or after the dye exhaustion just prior to boiling point.

SUPER MILLING DYES

L/R: 30:1   **Washfast quality:** good
pH level: 5.5–7 (weak acid)   **Lightfast quality:** good

Dye bath additives: Ammonium sulphate 3 gm to each 100 gm fibre (3%).

The method of dyeing is the same as that for Premetallized 1:2 dyes. See p. 68.

Handwoven wool floor or wall rug, dyed with fibre reactive and acid dyes.
Woven and dyed by Brian Milner.

Untitled handwoven tapestry in wool, silk and mohair, dyed with Ciba-Geigy Irgalan dyes.
Dyed and woven by Margery Blackman.

L/R: 30:1

pH level: 4.5–5

Washfast quality: good

Lightfast quality: good

Dye bath additives: Lyogen MF liquid as leveller.

Acetic acid to enable dye take up.

Glauber's salt for pale to medium shades. Use 5 gm to 100 gm of fibre (5%).

Dyeing method
1. Weigh the dry fibre to assess how much dye to use (refer pp.51–57). Make a paste with the dye using cold water, then pour double that amount of hot water over the paste and stir for two minutes. Set aside.
2. Prepare a dye bath of warm water at 50°C (122°F) and add acetic acid to give a pH reading of 4.5–5. Add 1% Lyogen MF (1ml to 100 gm of fibre) and Glauber's salt for pale shades.
3. Enter wet, clean fibre and soak it for 15 minutes.
4. Remove the fibre or push it to one side, add the dye, and stir well.
5. Raise the temperature to 98°C (208°F) over 45 minutes. Hold this for another 45 minutes.
6. Cool the fibre in the bath before removing it for rinsing. Fine fibres and silks may be kept at 80°C (180°F) for 60 minutes instead of simmering at stage 5.

PREMETALLIZED DYES

1:2 PREMETALLIZED DYES

L/R: 30:1

pH level: 5.5 (weak acid)

Washfast quality: good

Lightfast quality: good

Dye bath additives: 3% ammonium sulphate to release acid. Use 3 gm to each 100 gm of fibre, or use acetic acid.

Dyeing method
1. Weigh the dry fibre to assess how much dye to use (refer pp.51–57).
2. Prepare the dye bath and heat to 30°C (86°F).
3. Dissolve the ammonium sulphate in a little cold water and add it to the bath. Place the wetted fibre into the bath and let it soak for 20 minutes.
4. Remove the fibre and add the dye. Stir well and re-enter the fibre.
5. Bring the temperature to boiling slowly, over a period of 45 minutes. Rotate the fibre gently during dyeing. Retain the temperature for another 30 minutes to fix the dye.
6. Allow the fibre to cool in the bath. Wash in warm detergent water and rinse well.

An alternative recipe for Irgalan

This recipe uses different additives from the previous one. Albegal A is the levelling agent. Use 1% (1 ml to each 100gm fibre). Glauber's salt retards dyeing. Use 5 % (5 ml to each 100gm fibre). Acetic acid assists dye bond. A pH testing paper should read 5.5. This will be approximately 1 tbsp of 33 % acetic acid to 2 litres ($^1/2$ gallon) of water. Liquor ratio is 30:1.

Dyeing method

1. Heat the dye bath to 50°C (120°F) and stir in the additives. Dissolve the Glauber's salt in a little cold water before adding.
2. Enter the wetted fibre and allow it to soak in the liquid for 15 minutes.
3. Remove the fibre, or push it to one side, whilst adding the dissolved dye. Stir well, then re-enter the fibre.
4. Slowly increase the temperature to just below boiling and retain it for 30 minutes to allow dye fixation.

I find it equally as satisfactory to soak the washed fibre in warm water to which either Albegal A or a neutral liquid detergent has been added, before putting the fibre into the dye bath. For large amounts of fibre that are heavy to lift when wet, I prepare the dye bath, add the acetic acid and the dye liquid, and bring the termperature to 50°C, before adding the soaked fibre, and continue in the same manner as in the previous recipe.

Glauber's salt may be omitted, providing that the temperature rise is extremely slow, and the fibre is rotated regularly to prevent uneven dyeing.

BASIC DYES

TINFIX, SENNELIER

Washfast quality: poor   **Lightfast quality:** poor
Dye bath additives: Acetic acid.

To make 1 litre of dye liquid

1. Paste 0.5–1 gm of dye with cold water.
2. Add 250 ml (1 cup) of hot water and stir well.
3. Add 5 ml (1 tsp) of acetic acid (33% strength) or use the fixative recommended by the manufacturer.
4. Add 750 ml of warm water and stir.
5. Immerse the fibre or fabric into the dye bath and leave for 30–40 minutes, rotating regularly. Rinse well.

5. CHEMICAL DYE BATHS FOR CELLULOSE FIBRES

INTRODUCTION

Colour take up of dyes varies throughout the cellulose field. Rayon usually dyes to the darkest value, with unmercerised cotton usually being the lightest value. The weight of the woven fabric also has some bearing upon the final dye colour. Cotton fabrics include a wide range of weights, from voile, organdie, and lawn, through to poplin, denim, and canvas. See Chapter One for a more detailed discussion of cellulose fibre types.

Dyes designed for cellulose fibres also dye silk.

If your water is hard, the impurities affect the dye results, and it will be wise to use the water softener sodium hexame taphosphate, which is available at a chemist or drug store. To each litre of water, add 0.5 gm of softener. I recommend that you use this chemical in its pure form because proprietary brands may have bleach added which makes them unsuitable for use with dyes.

DYE TYPES SUITABLE FOR CELLULOSE FABRICS

In order to use this section on dyes you need to know into which major category your dye fits. The trade name of the dye is not quite so important. Find the section that refers to the same dye type as the dye you have, and you will find that it will react in the same manner.

Fibre reactive dyes

These are the most modern dyes and are most successful. They come in a good range of bright colours which are safe to use, economical, and easy to mix. Fibre reactive dyes react directly with the fibre: the dye is chemically fixed in an alkaline environment over a period of time to produce a permanent bond. For this reason the washfast and and lightfast qualities are excellent, and these have become the most used dyes.

The only drawbacks, which are easily overcome, are that once mixed with water the dye has a limited active life and, secondly, unreacted dye takes many rinses to completely remove all traces.

Fibre reactive dyes may be classed as 'cold' or 'hot'.

Cold dyes, ie Procion MX or Cibacron F, do not need to be heated. They are started with hand-hot water for a dye bath temperature of 40°C (105°F), and are therefore suitable for batik and other forms of resist.

Brand name	Manufacturer	Page reference
Procion MX	ICI	78
Cibacron F	Ciba-Geigy	81
Drimalan F	Sandoz	83
Drimarine K	Sandoz	83

Hot dyes, ie. Procion H, need some heating before reaction takes place completely at 80°C, 175°F.

Brand name	Manufacturer	Page reference
Procion H	ICI	85
Procion HE	ICI	85

Direct dyes

These are from an older class of dye. They are easy to use, but poorer washfast qualities have to be taken into consideration. For further information see p. 86.

Trade name	Manufacturer
Caprophenyl	Ciba-Geigy
Chlorantine	Ciba-Geigy
Diphenyl	Ciba-Geigy
Solophenyl	Ciba-Geigy
Chloramine	Sandoz
Diamin	Hoecht
Solar	Sandoz
Sirius	Bayer

Sulphur dyes

These are older synthetic dyes. Sulphur black is still widely used today. It is an excellent black – some dyers say 'the very best'. The other colours are rarely used. Washfast qualities are good, although boilfast qualities are only moderately so. For further information see p. 87.

Trade name	Manufacturer
Thional	ICI
Thionol	Sandoz

Vat dyes

All vat dyes can be applied to cellulose fibres, producing permanent colours that have excellent washfast and lightfast qualities and withstand bleaches, soaps, boiling water, and dry cleaning. Vat dyes require the use of rather unpleasant chemical assistants. For further information see p. 89.

Trade name	Manufacturer
Indanthren	Bayer
Cibanone	Ciba-Geigy
Caledon	ICI
Durindone	ICI
Sandothrene	Sandoz

Soluble Vat Dyes

These are suitable for dyeing cotton and other cellulose fibres, and also silk, viscose rayon and polyester. For further information see p. 90.

Trade name	Manufacturer
Soledon	ICI
Indigosol	Sandoz

Naphthol or azoic dyes

These dyes are used extensively in Indonesia for batik. They are a little more complicated to use than some dyes and need careful handling, but they produce very bright colours that are especially good in the range of reds, yellows, oranges and browns. However, their range of blues and greens is limited, with no turquoise and bright greens. Washfast and lightfast qualities are excellent. For further information see p. 91.

Trade name	Manufacturer
Azoic	Bayer
Ciba naphthol	Ciba-Geigy
Irga naphthol	Ciba-Geigy
Intramin	Hoechst
Azanil	Hoechst
Variamin	Hoechst
Brentamine	ICI
Brenthol	ICI

All purpose, household, or union dyes

These are readily available and simple to use. They are combination dyes suitable for a wide range of fibres. For further information see p. 94.

Trade name
Cushing Perfection
Deka L
Dylon
Fabdec
Fibrec
Putnam
Rit

Basic dyes

An early class of synthetic dye. A mordant is needed for dyeing cellulose fibres. These dyes are still used for dyeing flowers and rushes. Refer p. 74 for recipe (omit the acetic acid).

Trade name
Tinfix
Sennelier

FIBRE REACTIVE DYES

Dye baths using fibre reactive dyes involve three distinct stages.

Levelling

Either table salt (sodium chloride) or Glauber's salt (sodium sulphate) is used to reduce the solubility of the dye slightly, causing it to move around the fibre looking for a dye site and coating the fibres, promoting an even, or level dye. As the amount of dye increases, so does the amount of salt, therefore dark colours require more salt.

The dye is mixed with water and the wetted fibre is added, and stirred or moved. The salt is usually added gradually, in three equal stages, with the fibre having been removed each time before the addition and re-entered after stirring. The dye is not fixed at this stage. At higher temperatures more dye reacts with the water rather than with the fibre, and therefore 'hot' dyes such as Procion H, need more salt to make the dye less soluble.

Fixation

The second stage of the dye bath introduces the alkali, which raises the pH level thus enabling the reaction to take place. There is no more levelling at this stage, which shows the importance of the first stage.

Alkali used may be:
1. Soda ash. The purest form of sodium carbonate, available from dye distributors and chemical firms.
2. Washing soda. This is an impure form of soda ash, easily purchased at local stores.
3. Sodium bicarbonate. Baking soda.

Rinsing

1. Cold water to remove the salt.
2. Hot water and detergent to remove excess dye.
3. Several short cold rinses until the water runs clear, to remove excess dye.

PROCION MX

Washfast quality: excellent   **Lightfast quality:** excellent

Dye bath additives: Glauber's salt
Washing soda

Procion MX may be packaged and resold under a trade name, or may be part of a household or union dye such as Dylon or Pylam. This is a highly reactive dye – in other words, it reacts very fast. The temperature for reaction in a dye bath is 40°C, 105°F. No heat source is needed and a bucket may be the dye bath. Procion MX may be used for a dye bath or direct application (see Chapter Six).

Mix this dye a little at a time as you need it, for once it is mixed with water its active life is limited. In a dye bath the dye reacts with the fibre, the alkali and the water, and after four hours most of the dye will have reacted – even though the dye bath appears the same colour. You will find that even after an hour the dye bath will yield a much paler shade. The shelf life of the dye when mixed with water is 1–2 weeks, because although the reaction is slower in the absence of an alkali, the reaction between dye and water continues.

A 'long bath', indicating the length of time needed, is the most successful method of making a dye bath because it uses less dye powder, and produces a more level dye. Fixing is not needed after long bath dyeing, although steaming increases the temperature and often does improve the dye's washfast and lightfast qualities.

The 'short bath' method is initially faster for it uses more dye and very little water, in fact only enough to cover the fabric. Continual movement of the fibre through the liquid produces a level dye. The dye is finally fixed by heat, by either steaming, baking, ironing or batch ageing in polythene for a period of time. (See pp. 104–05.)

Procion MX Turquoise uses Glauber's salt, not table salt. Although the latter is satisfactory, results will be paler because there will be less reaction.

Long bath method

1. Weigh then prescour the fibre. Boil 30 minutes in detergent, using 2–4 ml detergent per litre of water. To the dye pot add warm water (40°C, 105°F – just above body temperature) to a liquor ratio of 30:1. For sample swatches the liquor ratio is 40:1.
2. Measure dye powder.

For each 100 gm of fibre use: 0.5 gm for pale shades
1.0 gm for medium shades
4.0 gm for deep shades

Mix the dye powder to a smooth paste with cold water. Take sufficient warm water from the dye bath to completely dissolve the powder and add this to the dye bath.

For dye solutions use:

$$\frac{W \times D}{S} = \frac{\text{fibre weight} \times \text{depth of shade required}}{\text{strength of dye solution}} = \text{Volume of dye solution}$$

3. Enter the wet, scoured fibre and stir frequently for 10 minutes.
4. Dissolve the salt in water taken from the dye bath. The amount used relates to the amount of dye used.

For pale shades use:	20% weight salt to fibre weight
For medium shades use:	50% weight salt to fibre weight
For deep shades use:	90% weight salt to fibre weight
For dark shades use:	110 % weight salt to fibre weight

Remove the fibre from the bath. Add the salt in three equal parts, at five minute intervals. Re-enter the fibre after each addition and stir frequently.

5. Fixing the dye. Measure the wash soda using 10% weight of soda to weight of fibre (ie. 10 gm soda per 100 gm fibre). Dissolve the soda in a small amount of warm water. Remove the fibre from the bath, and pour in the soda solution. Re-enter the fibre and rotate continually for 15–20 minutes.

6. Dye time. Leave the fibre in the bath for 1 hour. Stir it every 10 minutes.

   An alternative method for fabrics that need to be kept cool, ie waxed fabrics, is batch ageing. Lie the fabric or fibre on polythene. Cover with polythene and seal the edges to exclude the air. Leave for 2 hours and then rinse in cold water and dry slowly.

7. Rinsing. Rinse the fibre well in cold water. Several rinses will be needed until the water runs clear. Wash or boil in detergent solution using 3 ml detergent per litre of water ($1/2$ tsp per gallon). If boiling, simmer at 85°C, 190°F for 10 minutes. Remember silk should not be boiled.

Short bath method

This method uses more dye, less water and the salt is added all at once. Continual movement of the fibre is necessary to achieve a level dye. After dyeing, rinse well in cold water. The fibre is then either air dried out of direct sunlight for 12 hours, or the dye is heat fixed by steaming, ironing, dry baking, or batch ageing for 24 hours (see pp. 104–05). Fabrics or fibres are then washed in hot detergent water followed by several cool rinses.

1. Weigh the dry fibre. Liquor ratio is 5:1. Work out how many litres of water you will use. This recipe is for 1 litre.

2. Mix the dye. Use 3 gm (pale shades) – 15 gm (dark shades). Add just enough cold water to mix into a paste then add 250 ml (1 cup) of water at 60°C, 140°F (just above hand hot). Stir well until dissolved.

3. Dissolve the salt (180 gm (pale shades) – 270 gm (dark shades)) into 250 ml (1 cup) warm water. Add 250 ml of cold water. Stir this into the dye liquid which is then poured into the dye bath.

4. Add the fibre. A little more water may be needed to cover the fibre, which must be pushed continuously through the liquid for 6–10 minutes to force the dye through all of the fibre.

5. Dissolve 14 gm of wash soda in 250 ml of warm water. Lift the fibre from the dye bath and add the soda solution. Stir then re-enter the fibre. Dye time is 15 minutes, during which the fibre is regularly rotated.

6. Fixing. Batch age in polythene for 24 hours, or heat fix by steaming, ironing or dry baking, or dry naturally out of direct sunlight for 2 hours.

7. Rinse in cold water then wash in hot detergent water. Finally rinse again in cool water until all excess dye has been removed.

Short bath method suitable for a group or classroom

This dye method uses one solution of soda into which the fabrics are presoaked, and several dye baths of differing colours. This is suitable for dip dyes, tie dyes, folded or stitched fabrics and many other forms of resist. The fibres will need to be batch aged in polythene for 2 hours, or heat fixed by steaming, baking or ironing. (See pp. 104–05.) This method produces a dye that is not quite as level as the long bath method.

1. Clean the fibre ready for dyeing.
2. Presoak in the soda. Dissolve 40 gm soda (3 tbsp) in a little hot water and make this up to 3.5 litres (1 gallon) with cold water. Immerse the fabric and soak for 15 minutes.
3. Make the dye solutions. Paste the dye with a little cold water, then add sufficient hot water to completely dissolve the dye . Make this up to 1 litre (1 quart) with warm water.

For pale shades use:	15 gm (5 tsp) dye
For dark shades use:	30 gm (10 tsp) dye
For very small amounts use:	0.25 gm (¼ tsp) dye for pale shades
	3 gm (3 tsp) dye for dark shades

Paste the dye as usual and make the liquid up to 250 ml (1 cup) in volume.
4. Add the salt to the dye solution. Multiply the weight of the dye x 10 to find the weight of salt to be added, ie 30 gm (1 tbsp) salt to each 3 gm (1 tsp) dye powder. Dissolve this in a little hot water and add it to the dye solution.
5. Squeeze out the excess soda solution from the fibre and either:
(a) Dip the fibre into the dye + salt solution, making sure that there is sufficient liquid to cover the fibre fully, and leave until the desired depth of colour is achieved; or
(b) Remove sufficient dye + salt solution from the container to paint, spray, or sponge the dye over the fibre. This prevents the dye from being contaminated with the soda, and the dye bath will last longer.
   If option (a) is taken the dye bath will be exhausted after 2 hours.
6. Fixing. Batch age in plastic for 2 hours then dry naturally before rinsing; or steam small pieces for 3 minutes and large pieces for 8 minutes.
7. Rinse. If bound resists have been used, leave the bindings on during the first rinsing to prevent any 'bleeding' of unreacted dye into adjacent areas. Rinse in repeated cold rinses. Wash in hot detergent water then rinse in cool water.
   Fabrics or fibres may be redyed by soaking again in the soda solution, before reapplying the dye. You may like to try soaking the fabric in the soda solution and then allowing it to dry before painting it with a dye + salt solution.

CIBACRON F

Washfast quality: excellent   **Lightfast quality:** excellent

Dye bath additives: Glauber's salt
                        Soda ash or wash soda
                        Albegal FFD as a wetting agent

This is a highly reactive dye, but a little less so than Procion MX. This gives it a greater stability in water and unreacted dye is slightly easier to wash out. The shelf life of this dye, once mixed with water, is consequently extended to 4–12 weeks.

The dye is classed as a cold dye, because it is started with warm water and requires no further heating for reaction to take place. The temperature recommended for these dyes is usually 40°C, 105°F. Slightly better results are achieved if the temperature is raised to 60°C, 140°F when dyeing in a home situation using soda ash or wash soda as the alkali. This temperature is, however, too hot for silk, which should be dyed at a temperature no higher than 48°C, 120°F.

Ciba-Geigy recommends its wetting agent Albegal FFD, which is similar to liquid detergent, to be used in conjunction with Cibacron F dyes. You will note that this dye uses more salt than Procion MX.

Long bath method

The temperature that I use for this recipe is 48°C 120°F so it will therefore be satisfactory for cellulose fibres and for silk. This is just above body temperature and the water from your hot water tap should be approximately correct. The temperature may be raised to 60°C,140°F for cotton.

1. Weigh the fibre. Prepare the fibre for dyeing. To a dye pot add warm water at 48°C. 120°F with a liquor ratio of 30:1.
2. Measure dye powder.

For each 100 gm of fibre use: 0.5 gm for pale shades
1.0 gm for medium shades
4.0 gm for deep shades

Mix the dye powder to a smooth paste with cold water. Take sufficient warm water from the dye bath to completely dissolve the powder and add this to the dye bath.

For dye solutions use:

$$\frac{W \times D}{S} = \frac{\text{fibre weight} \times \text{depth of shade required}}{\text{strength of dye solution}} = \text{Volume of dye solution}$$

Add this quantity of dye solution to the dye bath.

3. Dissolve the salt in water taken from the dye bath. The amount of salt relates to the amount of dye used. Add the salt to the dye bath and mix well.

For pale shades use	60% weight of salt to fibre weight.
For medium shades use	90% weight of salt to fibre weight.
For dark shades use	120% weight of salt to fibre weight.
For very dark shades use	140% weight of salt to fibre weight.

4. Squeeze excess water from the fibre and put it into the dye bath. Stir very well, and continue to move the fibre frequently as the temperature is held for 45 minutes.
5. Dissolve the soda ash or wash soda (sodium carbonate) in a small amount of warm water. Use 10% weight of soda to weight of fibre, ie 10 gm soda to 100

gm of fibre. Remove the fibre from the bath and pour the soda solution into the dye bath. Stir well and re-enter the fibre.
6. Dye time. Rotate the fibre regularly for 45 minutes. The dyed fibre may also be batch aged or fixed by steaming, instead of this dye time.
7. Rinsing. Rinse in cold water until excess dye has been removed. Wash in hot water to which detergent has been added. Ciba-Geigy recommends Synthrapol. Cotton and linen may be boiled for 10 minutes at 85°C (190°F). Rinse well in warm water.

DRIMALAN F AND DRIMARINE K

Washfast quality: excellent   **Lightfast quality:** excellent

Dye bath additives: Glauber's salt or common salt
                       Soda ash or wash soda

These are also fibre reactive dyes which work best at a temperature of 60°C (140°F). Glauber's salt (sodium sulphate), or common salt (sodium chloride) force the dye into the fibre, and soda ash or wash soda is the alkali used.

Dye bath method
1. Weigh the fibre and prescour it ready for dyeing. To a dye pot add hand-hot water (40–50°C, 104–122°F) at a liquor ratio of 30:1.
2. Measure dye powder.

For each 100 gm of fibre use: 0.5 gm for pale shades
                                         1.0 gm for medium shades
                                         4.0 gm for deep shades

Mix the dye powder to a smooth paste with cold water. Take sufficient warm water from the dye bath to completely dissolve the powder and add this to the dye bath.

For dye solutions use:

$$\frac{W \times D}{S} = \frac{\text{fibre weight} \times \text{depth of shade required}}{\text{strength of dye solution}} = \text{volume of dye solution}$$

Add this quantity of dye solution to the dye bath.

3. Add the wet fibre and stir frequently for 20 minutes.
4. Remove the fibre from the dye bath. Dissolve the Glauber's salt in a little warm water before adding it to the pot in three equal portions at 5 minute intervals. Re-enter the fibre after each addition and stir frequently.

The amount of Glauber's salt relates to the amount of liquid in the dye bath.

For pale shades use:	20 gm Glauber's salt to 1 litre water
For pale/medium use:	30 gm Glauber's salt to 1 litre water
For medium shades use:	40 gm Glauber's salt to 1 litre water
For dark shades use:	60 gm Glauber's salt to 1 litre water.

Common salt (sodium chloride) may be used instead of Glauber's salt, using the same weight to each litre of water.

5. Increase the temperature slowly over a period of 30 minutes, until 60°C (140°F) is reached. Stir or rotate the fibre regularly during this time.

6. Add alkali (soda ash or wash soda) to fix the dye. Remove the fibre before adding the soda and return it after stirring.

The amount of alkali relates to the amount of water in the dye pot.

For pale shades use:	2 gm per litre of water
For dark shades use:	5–10 gm per litre of water

Rotate the fibre regularly, maintaining the dye bath temperature at approximately 60°C (140°F) for 15 minutes for pale shades, 45 minutes for dark shades.

7. Cool the dye bath over a period of 20 minutes before removing the fibre.

8. Rinsing. Overflow with cold running water for 2 minutes to remove all excess dye. Wash in warm detergent water, then wash again in very hot water to which detergent has been added. Rinse in warm water, then finally rinse again in cold water.

When rinsing silk, add 1 gm of sodium bicarbonate per litre of water to the first detergent wash and soak for 30 minutes in this warm water. Omit the hot wash.

Drimarene Turquoise K and **Drimarene Brilliant Green K** need to be taken to a temperature of 80°C (176°F) which is held for 40 minutes.

For pale shades use:	10–40 gm of salt to each litre of water
	1 gm of soda ash to each 100 gm of fibre
For medium shades use:	40–60 gm of salt to each litre of water
	2 gm of soda ash to 100 gm of fibre
For deep shades use:	60–80 gm of salt to each litre of water
	2–4 gm of soda for each 100 gm of fibre

Mix the salt and soda together.

To a dye bath containing the fibre and the dye, add ⅙ of the salt/soda mixture and stir for 20 minutes. Add ²⁄₆ (⅓) salt/soda and stir for 20 minutes, then add the remaining mixture. After 20 minutes start to raise the temperature to 80°C (176°F).

Washfast quality: excellent   **Lightfast quality:** excellent

Dye bath additives: Soda ash or wash soda

These are called the 'hot' dyes because they require heat to enable the reaction to take place. 'H' stands for 'heat' and 'E' stands for 'exhaust', suggesting that this dye is most suitable for exhaust dyeing.

The dye is a slow reacting dye, which makes it very suitable for textile printing since the slower reaction reduces the amount of 'bleeding' of the dye. It is also suitable for dyeing more difficult, tougher or tightly woven fabrics, or yarns that have been tightly spun.

The temperature at which reaction takes place is 80°C (175°F), which is above room temperature, and the dye bath therefore needs to be heated. Liquor ratio is 30:1.

Dye bath method

1. Weigh the dry fibre and prescour ready for dyeing. To a dye pot add warm water, approximately 40°C (105°F), which is just above body temperature.
2. Measure dye powder.

For each 100 gm of fibre use: 0.5 gm for pale shades
                                                     1 gm for light shades
                                                     2 gm for medium shades
                                                     4 gm for deep shades

Mix the dye powder to a smooth paste with cold water. Take sufficient warm water from the dye bath to completely dissolve the powder and add this to the dye bath.

For dye solutions use:

$$\frac{W \times D}{S} = \frac{\text{fibre weight x depth of shade required}}{\text{strength of dye solution}} = \text{Volume of dye solution}$$

3. Measure the salt in relation to the amount of dye used and the desired shade.

For pale shades use: 80 gm salt to 100 gm of fibre
For light/medium shades use: 120 gm salt to 100 gm of fibre.
For medium/dark shades use: 150 gm salt to 100 gm of fibre.
For dark shades use: 200 gm salt to 100 gm of fibre.

Dissolve the salt in a little warm water taken from the dye pot. Add one third of the salt to the dye pot and stir well.

4. Enter the fibre/fabric or yarn after it has been thoroughly wetted in warm water. Increase the temperature to 80°C (175°F) and maintain this for 20 minutes stirring frequently.

5. Remove the fabric and add the second third of the salt. Five minutes later add the final third. The fibre is removed while the salt is added, then re-entered.

6. Add the soda. Using either wash soda or soda ash, dissolve it in a small amount of warm water taken from the dye bath. Remove the fibre and pour in the soda. Stir well and re-enter the fibre. Rotate the fibre and maintain the temperature of 80°C (175°F) for 45 minutes. Use 30% weight of soda to weight of fibre, ie. 30 gm per 100 gm fibre.

7. Rinsing. Begin with a cold water rinse, then wash, or boil in hot water to which liquid detergent has been added to a rate of 3 ml to each litre of water ($^1/2$ tsp per1 gallon). Bring to the boil then simmer for 15 minutes. Finally give several warm rinses.

DIRECT DYES

Direct dyes are from an older class of dye, so called because they need no mordant and therefore dye the fabric directly. They are sometimes called **application** dyes. They are very similar to the acid levelling dyes for animal fibres, but are designed for use on cellulose fibres. They also dye silk and viscose rayon.

Direct dyes are easy to use because they are soluble in water and are easily mixed. They require the addition of common salt to improve colour take-up. The colour range is extensive including a dark black. The dyes are also inexpensive.

Although the lightfast qualities of direct dyes are excellent, the washfast qualities are only moderate and they are therefore not suitable for items that require frequent washing. Fixatives which complement certain dyes improve the washfast qualities. For instance, Deka L series uses Fixative III, which is applied after washing and rinsing.

The most suitable temperature for this dye to give the best results, is 85–90°C (185–194°F). This is too high for silk and for batik waxes, and therefore the dye bath needs to be brought to this temperature and then cooled until a temperature more suitable for the fabric or wax is reached.

When using these dyes to dye silk, wool or any other animal fibres, salt is omitted from the dye bath and acetic acid or white vinegar is substituted. If these dyes are used for silk, steaming will be required to heat fix the dyes.

Mixed dyes can be stored for later use without deterioration.

I do advise that you read the instructions accompanying the dye, in order to find out what weight of fabric the dye in the container or sachet will successfully colour. The intensity of the final shade will depend upon the fabric or fibre being clean, wetted before immersion in the dye bath, receiving sufficient dye time, and the correct concentration of dye.

DEKA L

Deka L dyes are probably the most extensively used direct dyes. They contain both direct dyes and acid dyes and may therefore also be classed as a **union** or **household** dye. The fixative recommended by the manufacturer (Fixative III) improves washfastness.

General dyeing of cotton, linen and viscose rayon

Ensure that the fibre is clean, free from size, and thoroughly wetted before dyeing. Liquor ratio is a little less than 30:1 (30 ml to 1 gm fibre).

1. Mix the dye. The dye distributors recommend that 10 gm dye powder will dye 240 gm (8 oz) fabric to a medium dark shade. Paste the dye with a little cold water. Into the dye pot put 5 litres (1 gallon) of warm water. Add the dye and stir until completely dissolved.
2. Add the salt to the dye pot and stir well. The weight of salt required is 20% of the weight of the fibre. Use 50 gm (2 tbsp) for 240 gm fabric.
3. Enter the wetted fabric and rotate frequently.
4. Increase the temperature. Over a period of 15 minutes, raise the temperature to 85–90°C (185–194°F). Stir continuously.
5. Hold the temperature for 30 minutes.
6. Rinse until the water runs clear.
7. Fixative. One packet of approximately 10 gm will treat 450 gm (1 lb) of fabric. Dissolve the fixative in 1 litre of boiling water, then add 5 litres of cold water. The temperature should be 20–25°C (70–80°F). Air the fabric without rinsing the fixative out. When it is completely dry, wash and rinse the fabric. Although humidity may harden the fixative, it is not impaired.

A dye solution suitable for batik, tie dye, and silk

This recipe is for a stronger solution, using 10 gm of dye powder, and dyeing 150 gm (5 oz) of fabric to a medium shade.

1. Make a paste with 10 gm of dye and a little warm water.
2. Add 25 gm salt for cotton, other cellulose fibres and rayon, or 2 tbsp white vinegar for silk, wool and animal fibres.
3. Cover with 2–3 litres of boiling water, and stir well. Leave this to cool to 50°C (125°F).
4. Immerse the fabric and stir frequently for 30–45 minutes.
5. Rinse well.

Fixative may be used after rinsing. Heat-steaming or ironing will also help to improve washfastness.

SULPHUR DYES (SULPHUR BLACK)

Sulphur dyes have a small range of dull, dark colours, such as brown, navy, khaki, and black. The dyes are insoluble in water but soluble in the presence of Glauber's salt (sodium sulphite) and they are oxidised after dyeing, either by airing or by the use of oxidising agents such as sodium bichromate or hydrogen peroxide.

The New Zealand distributors of sulphur dyes sell the preparation Leucad SH, which is sodium sulphahydrate and sodium hydrosulphide, which de-oxygenates the dye bath. They state that glucose could be substituted. They also sell a wetting agent, Rewin W, which is stable at a high pH level and has been designed for use with sulphur dyes.

The chemicals used in this recipe are very caustic and need most careful handling in a well ventilated situation. The amounts used are a percentage weight of the fibre.

To dye 100 gm of fibre
1. Fill the dye bath with warm water at 40°C (100°F) and enter the wet fibre and leave it to soak for 10 minutes.
2. Lift out the fibre and add the dye.

For dark shades use: 20% liquid dye (20 ml or 4 tsp) *or* 10% dye powder (10 gm or 2 tsp)
For light shades use: 16% liquid dye (16 ml or 3 tsp) *or* 8% dye powder (8 gm or $1^1/2$ tsp)

Re-enter the fibre and maintain the temperature for 10 minutes.
3. Remove the fibre. Add 2% caustic soda (2 gm) to a cup of **cold** water, stir until dissolved then add it to the dye bath.

Add 10% sodium sulphahydrate (10 gm or 2 tsp) or Leucad SH. This may also be dissolved first into a cup of cold water.

Re-enter the fibre. The dye bath temperature is maintained at 40°C (100°F) for 15 minutes more.
4. Raise the temperature to 80°C (175°F) and maintain this for 15 minutes.
5. Add 10% Glauber's salt (10 gm or 2 tsp) and retain the temperature at 80°C (175°F) for 10 minutes.
6. Rinse the fibre very briefly in cold running water until the water is clear.
7. Prepare a bath of warm water (50°C, 120°F) and to it add 2% of hydrogen peroxide (2 ml or less than $^1/2$ tsp). Enter the fibre and leave it for 15 minutes, keeping the bath at this temperature.
8. Neutralise the bath by adding 2ml of 33% acetic acid and leave it for a further 15 minutes. Rotate the fibre regularly. The fibre may now be washed in hot water to which 4 ml or 1 tsp of Rewin W or a liquid detergent has been added.

Sulphur Black may be used to **cold pad batch** by mixing the chemicals together with the dye and allowing the liquid to cool before applying directly to the fibre, which is then covered with polythene to exclude the air and left to batch for four hours in a warm situation (30°C, 85°F). A warm sunny room or an airing cupboard is satisfactory. The fibre is then rinsed in cold water and washed in very hot water to which 4 ml of Rewin W or liquid detergent has been added.

Padding mixture
100 ml Sulphur Black liquid or 50 gm powder
200 gm Leucad SH or sodium sulphahydrate
25 gm common salt (sodium chloride)

Dissolve together in 400 ml ($1^1/2$ cups) of boiling water.

VAT DYES

Vat dyes are insoluble in water and need to be changed in form before they will dye fibres. In a strong alkali solution of caustic soda and sodium hydrosulphite, oxygen is removed, and the dye then becomes soluble, and can be applied to fibre. When the fibre + dye are exposed to the air, oxidization converts the dye back to the insoluble stage which is then permanently fixed to the fibre. In the alkali solution the dye appears to have no colour or no colour related to the final oxidized shade.

Indigo is an ancient vat dye originally derived naturally from plants, but synthetic indigo is usually used today. The recipe for natural indigo on pp. 45–46 may be used for any of the synthetic vat dyes.

The rather unpleasant chemical assistants used for vat dyeing need very careful handling.

Here is a recipe for dyeing cotton, other cellulose fibres and viscose rayon with vat dyes, which is a little easier to follow than the more precise recipe in Chapter Two.

Put on your rubber gloves, protective clothing and a face mask. You will need a container which will hold 1 litre and is not made of metal. Glass would be excellent.

Method
1. Weigh the fibre to be dyed, then scour it ready for dyeing.
2. Measure the dye powder and chemical assistants.

100 gm of fibre requires:	5 gm dye
	10 gm caustic soda
	10 gm sodium hydrosulphite

3 Paste the dye powder with water or a little methylated spirit, then add 200 ml (^{4}/5 cup) of hot water. Stir well.
4. Into a small amount of **cold** water, add half of the caustic soda, ie 5 gm, and dissolve it completely. Add this to the dye.
5. Scatter half of the hydrosulphite, ie 5 gm, onto the top of the dye and stir until dissolved.
6. Leave this to stand for 10 minutes.
5. Prepare the dye bath with sufficient water to cover the fabric. Add the dye solution. Dissolve the second portion (5 gm) of caustic soda into a little **cold** water then add it to the dye bath. Add the remaining hydrosulphite, stirring very gently.

To dye the fabric
Immerse the wetted fabric and push it gently beneath the surface of the dye liquid for 10 minutes. Avoid making bubbles of air and do not allow the fabric above the surface.

Oxidize by lifting the fabric and allowing it to drip and then hanging it out of direct sunlight for 15 minutes. Rinse in cold water until the water runs clear. Finally wash it in warm detergent water and rinse well.

Black and blue dyes require a stronger alkali solution for a good depth of colour. I suggest that you double the quantities of caustic soda and sodium hydrosulphite when dyeing these shades.

SOLUBLE VAT DYES

Indigosol is the dye most commonly used by the home dyer in this part of the world. It is a cold water soluble dye with good washfast and lightfast qualities. However, great care needs to be used when dyeing with Indigosol because although the dyes will develop in light with heat, they are usually developed in a bath of hydrochloric acid, and sodium nitrate.

The dyes are colourless until oxidized, and they are suitable for dyeing cotton and other cellulose fibres and also silk, viscose rayon and polyester.

Dye bath method

Two baths are prepared, the first containing the dye and the second containing the chemical developer. The two baths are **never** mixed. Dye solutions may be stored in the dark for a month if necessary.

1. Prepare the dye by dissolving it in a little hot water, approximately 60°C (140°F). Use 2–3 gm of dye to each litre of water for a medium shade (2–3 tsp to a quart). Make sufficient solution to amply cover the fibre.
2. Prepare the developer with extreme care because the chemicals are dangerous. Wear a face mask and do not inhale the fumes. Wear rubber gloves and avoid splashing. Always add the acid to the water.

    To each litre (quart) of **cold** water add 20 ml of hydrochloric acid, one drop at a time. To this add 1 gm of sodium nitrate.
3. Immerse the clean wetted fabric into the first bath containing the dye, making sure that it is well submerged. Leave it for 5 minutes for pale shades and 15 minutes for strong shades. Lift the fabric from the bath and hang it out to drip away the excess for a few minutes.
4. Immerse the fabric into the second developing bath and the colour will develop. Do not inhale the fumes.
5. Lay the cloth in the sun, away from shadows, and turn over every few minutes. Maximum colour should be achieved within 5–15 minutes.
6. Rinse in cold running water until all traces of acid have gone. Test with pH paper for neutral.

Dye procedure may be repeated several times to produce deeper shades. The useful life of a dye bath is between four and five hours.

Direct application

The dyes may be used for painting and other forms of direct application by mixing 3–4 gm (3–4 tsp) of dye powder to 100 ml ($^1/_3$ cup) water and applying. Allow this to dry naturally, them draw the fabric through the second developing bath of hydrochloric acid and sodium nitrate and continue as for dip dyeing.

See also Inkodye vat dye, p.111.

NAPHTHOL OR AZOIC DYES

Naphthol dyes require two separate baths which must **never** be mixed together. The safest method of identification is to label each one. The first bath is the naphthol bath to saturate the fibre. To this bath an alkali is added, usually caustic soda (sodium hydroxide), to make the dye soluble.

The second bath contains the colour salts, called **diazo** salts, which react with the naphthol in the fibre to give an instantaneous, permanent colour. Naphthol dyes require no steam or heat fixing.

Colour

Naphthols for the first bath have coded letters and diazo salts for the second bath have colour identification. The colour that you achieve depends upon which naphthol is used with which salt. You may use one naphthol base with different salts, or vice versa. Experimentation, with notes and samples, is the best form of learning.

Here is an example:

Naphthol AS with Diazo salt Red B produces light crimson.
Naphthol AS BO with Diazo salt Red B produces maroon.
Naphthol AS LB with Diazo salt Red B produces red brown.

These are some choices of naphthols:

Naphthol AS G produces yellow with most salts.
GR produces green with blue salts.
LB produces browns with all salts.
SR produces grey to black on cotton.
TR used for pastel shades.
BO used for strong colours.

These naphthols generally produce the colours described by the salt:
D, OL, RS, AS, AS D, BS.

Diazo salts may be mixed together providing that the ratio of naphthol to salt is retained at 1:2. The name indicates the expected colour range. The choices include: Red B, Scarlet GG, Blue B, Blue BB, Violet B, Bordeaux GP, Orange RD, Green BB, Black K, BTL, and ANS, and Yellow GL.

Storage of naphthols and diazo salts

Keep them out of direct light and protect them from moisture.

Dye bath method

A standard recipe uses, to each litre of water:

For very pale shades:	0.5 gm naphthol / 1 gm diazo salt
For light shades:	1 gm naphthol / 2 gm diazo salt

| *For medium shades:* | 2 gm naphthol / 4 gm diazo salt |
| *For dark shades:* | 3 gm naphthol / 6 gm diazo salt |

Depth of colour is achieved by increasing the amount of naphthol and diazo salt, or by repeating the two baths in order, rinsing between dip dyes.

Equipment
Each bath needs separate utensils because they should not be mixed in any way. You will need two dye baths, labelled to avoid confusion, two plastic or glass measuring jugs and two spoons. Shallow baths are best and plastic baths are excellent and inexpensive. Do not use metal.

Accurate weighing of naphthols and salts is important, so you need scales.

When you begin dyeing, make sure that you have boiling water and a bottle of the alkali sodium hydroxide solution ready at hand.

Mix the alkali solution
1. Measure 441 gm caustic soda (sodium hydroxide) and carefully **add to** one litre of **cold** water.
2. Stir until dissolved.

Mix the solution very slowly and carefully and store in a dark bottle, with a plastic or cork stopper. Label it very clearly and store out of children's reach.

As the common name suggests, sodium hydroxide is caustic to skin, to work areas and to clothing. Wear rubber gloves and avoid splashing. If the solution comes into contact with the skin, wash the area immediately with copious amounts of cold water.

Caustic soda is often referred to by the Indonesian word 'loog'. When mixing the naphthol baths, have this loog ready at hand to add immediately to the bath.

Mix the naphthol bath
1. For a medium shade of dye, measure 2 gm of naphthol powder into a plastic or glass jug. Mix this to a paste by adding a little methylated spirit or turkey red oil (TRO). Boiling water may also be used to paste.
2. Add 250 ml boiling water (1 cup) and stir well to dissolve the powder. Immediately add caustic soda loog one drop at a time, until the naphthol is clear and yellow. The amount of loog may vary from 5–20 ml but is generally 1.5–2 ml to each gram of naphthol. Use no more than necessary and work fast to keep the solution near boiling point. If the naphthol does not clear when the loog is added, it may be reheated and stirred. Naphthol SR will not become clear.
3. Cool the naphthol bath for 5 minutes then add sufficient cold water to make it up to 1 litre. Keep the naphthol bath out of direct sunlight.

Mix the diazo salt bath
For a medium shade of dye, measure 4 gm of salt powder and mix it to a paste with a little cold water. Add more cold water to make it up to 1 litre.

To dye
1. Prescour the fabric to remove starches, dirt or sizes. Iron it if necessary. Wet the fibre for 10–20 minutes.
2. Put on your rubber gloves. Place the entire cloth in the naphthol bath and draw the fabric gently through the bath. Lift the cloth and allow the drips to fall back into the bath. Take the fabric away and hang it up to drip for 10 minutes, out of direct sunlight. Any naphthol that drips into the diazo salt bath exhausts the dye.
3. Place the fabric into the salt bath, agitate a little, then draw it gently through the bath. Leave the cloth in the bath for 5 minutes. Hang out again until it has stopped dripping, then rinse it in cold running water until it runs clear. Baths 1 and 2 may be repeated if required for a deeper shade. Finally wash or boil in hot soapy water.

Patchy dyeing may result from one of the following:
• The fabric is not completely wet before dyeing.
• Insufficient scouring to remove starches, dirt, and size.
• The fabric has not been passed evenly through the baths.
• The colour salts have been exhausted from bath 2.

The useful life of the dye bath is approximately six hours before it deteriorates. The diazo bath is exhausted when it appears cloudy, containing insoluble dye particles. Mix a new one if dyeing is not yet completed.
Some dyers neutralize all naphthol in the fabric before entering it into the diazo salt bath by immersing the fabric in a sodium chloride (common salt) bath. Dissolve 2 tbsp of salt in 1 litre of hot water then make it up to 5 litres with cold water. Merely draw the fabric through the salt bath, rinse it, allow excess water to drip out, then continue to the diazo salt bath in the usual manner.

Direct application
1. Dip the fabric into the naphthol + loog bath and then allow it to dry completely in the air. Avoid direct sunlight on the fabric.
2. Mix a concentrated diazo salt solution and use this to paint, sponge, spray or drip onto the fabric. Use 2 gm salt to 125 ml of water (2 tsp–1/2 cup). Dry completely by hanging the fabric in the shade.
3. Wash it in very hot water to which washing soda has been added. To each 1 litre of water add 4 ml (4 tsp) soap and 2 gm (2 tsp) of wash soda.

Dyeing silk and wool
Naphthol dyes may be used on animal fibres, although the results may be different. The protein of the animal fibre reacts with the diazo salt and the colours produced are a little yellower than on cellulose. Caustic soda used in the naphthol bath will also damage the fibres, so shades using the minimum of loog are recommended.
Add 2 ml of white vinegar, or very weak acetic acid, to each litre of diazo salt bath (1/2 tsp per quart). This will reduce the alkalinity slightly.

ALL PURPOSE / HOUSEHOLD / UNION DYES

These dyes are expensive because they are a combination of dyes for both protein and cellulose fibres and the unused portions are washed away and wasted. They may also have the salt and alkali already added. They are, however, readily available from chemist shops and stores.

Directions are simple and usually supplied with the dye. Read the instructions carefully to find out how much dye powder or liquid you need to dye your weight of fibre.

Dye bath method

1. Stir the dye into a small amount of hot water, then make it up to the required amount with warm water. Thoroughly wet the fibre before putting it into the dye bath.

2. Simmer the dye bath just below boiling point and agitate or rotate the fibre frequently for 30 minutes.

    The simmer temperature is not suitable for wool or silk. For these fibres use a much cooler dye bath and rotate the fibre whilst the bath is cool, ceasing as the temperature rises.

3. After dyeing is completed, cool rinse the fabric, then air dry it. Once dry, wash it again in hot water to which a detergent has been added, then follow with several warm rinses.

• **Dylon** may be used in the same manner as Procion MX, including the 'cold' bath methods.

• **Deka L** instructions are found in the section on direct dyes (p. 86).

6. DIRECT APPLICATION OF CHEMICAL DYES

Direct application methods using 'cold' dyes enable you to place a concentrated dye exactly where you want it on yarn, fibre or fabric. (For a more detailed discussion of different techniques see Chapter Seven.) Heating is not required because the dyes fix at a warm room temperature over a period of time, or by the direct application of heat.

It is not possible to assess exactly how much dye to use and experience, sight and intuition will suggest the amount.

Urea, which is produced from natural gas, is used in most direct application methods. It suspends the dye and helps to delay drying, which gives the necessary time needed to fix the dye to the fibre.

For painting and spraying, the dye does not need to be thickened, but if you want to squeeze the dye from a bottle, or you do not want it to spread so far across the fibre, you may prefer to thicken it. Screen printing or block printing also requires a much thicker dye paste than other direct application methods. The thickener or 'padding' also supports the dye, prevents it from drying out and therefore extends the fixing time.

Sodium alginate, used for thickening, was originally derived from seaweeds. It swells in water, does not affect the dye and washes out easily. Trade names include Manutex and Keltex. Polycell wallpaper paste is also sodium alginate and although it contains other additives it makes a good substitute. Use the one that does not contain fungicide.

When mixed, this stock paste can be kept for months in a refrigerator (it may mould at room temperature). Label it well for safety reasons.

THE DYES

As we have seen, some dyes are designed specifically for cellulose fibres or fabrics; others for protein. Some, such as Procion MX, may be used for protein or cellulose fibres and fabrics, providing care is taken to include all the necessary additives and to achieve the correct degree of acidity for animal fibres. As before, if you match your fibre to the appropriate section you will find specific directions for your dye or general directions for your dye type. Dyes requiring the same temperature, the same conditions and the same additives may be mixed together – in other words, keep the dyes within the same series of dye types.

Dyes are now available in liquid form containing all the necessary additives and ready for immediate use as cold water dyes. They may be thickened if required. Earth Palette, an Australian dye, fits this description in the protein dyeing section, as does Inkodye vat dye in the cellulose section.

DIRECT APPLICATION ON PROTEIN FIBRES

Dye may be applied directly to protein fibres using fibre reactive dyes together with acid and a wetting agent. The fibre is usually batch aged in polythene for 24–48 hours to fix the dye (see p.102). Oven baking may also be considered as a fixation method.

COLD PAD BATCH DYEING

More precise dyeing can be achieved by suspending the dyes in a cold pad. 'Cold pad batch' means that the dyes are 'cold'; a 'pad' means a thickened mixture in which to suspend the dyes; and 'batch age' means that the fibre is wrapped in plastic or polythene sheeting to exclude the air, and left to 'age' for 24–48 hours. At the time of writing, only fibre reactive dyes could be used in this manner.

Equipment

The equipment is minimal – rubber gloves to protect the hands; a face mask for handling dry dye powders; a container in which to mix the padding mixture; a large table covered with polythene sheeting and newspapers, and polythene sheeting in which to fold the fibre. Small beakers or plastic cups and small jam jars, are all useful when mixing the dyes.

A collection of painting brushes, perhaps a roller or a paint spray, a plastic drainpipe around which you could bind yarns so that individual threads can be painted, will all soon be collectable items.

Acid levels

The pH level for wool dyes is 5.0–5.5, and I always use pH testing papers. I have found that the blue and violet shades, as well as the Cibacrolan dyes, need more acetic acid for a pH level of 4.5.

Chemical assistants

The chemical assistants are readily available.

- Sodium alginate thickeners such as Manutex are used for the 'pad', but Polycell craft paste without the fungicide is a good substitute. Methylated spirit makes it easier to mix. Once made, the padding mixture may be stored in a refrigerator for many months.
- The leveller, or wetting agent, is the one that you usually use for your dye.
- Urea is used to swell the fibre and assists the dye to transfer to the fibre. It is easy to find at most garden supply shops.

Mixing colours

One small drawback with this method is that it is not a precise method of mixing dye colours. Trial, error and experience will enable you to know how much dye to use, with what amount of padding mixture. By using percentage dye solutions and keeping records, I have been able to achieve very close colour matches by recording the percentage of dye used to padding mixture. Most of the time I judge by 'eye', or I paint a small sample length. Remember that it will be a lighter shade when dry. If a colour is too weak, add more dye. If it is too strong, add more padding mixture.

Another point to consider is that the dye spreads along the fibre, and colours painted beside each other will overlap and mix. This, of course, leads to many exciting permutations of colour, but if it isn't what you want, leave a space between the dyes when applying them.

'Sunset'. A colour study by Ann Milner. Painted cotton tape, handwoven.

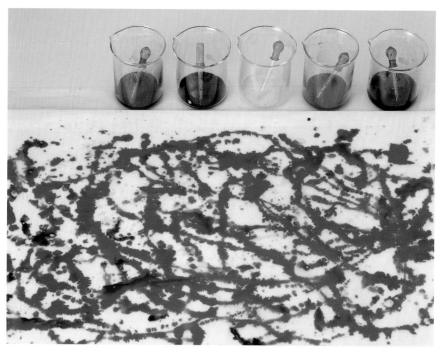

Silk is painted with padding mixture then dye, to which acid has been added, is squirted on to the surface.

The painted silk is covered very carefully with a sheet of plastic or polythene. The dyes are pushed beneath the plastic so that they merge with one another. This is left in a warm situation for 24 hours before washing out the dyes.

Two silk scarves dyed using the cold pad method.

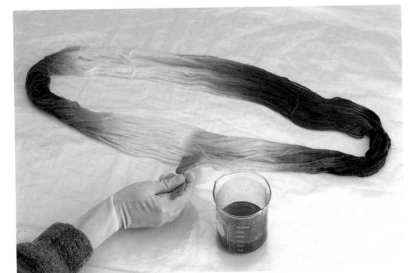

Cold pad batch a skein of yarn by mixing the dyes into padding mixture and painting them on with a brush, Leave clear areas between colours into which the dyes can 'bleed'.

Remove the towels and cover the yarn with polythene.

Roll the polythene and yarn and seal the edges to exclude air. Leave it to 'age' for 24 hours in a warm situation.

Recipe for 1 litre of padding mixture

I find this amount sufficient to paint 200 gm of hanked yarn. I usually add the acetic acid immediately before adding the mixture to the dyes.

1. Dissolve the urea. Measure 500 ml (2 cups) of water at 40°C (105°F) into a container. Add 300 gm of urea and stir well. The temperature reduces rapidly and you may need to heat the solution to dissolve the urea fully.
2. Thickening agent. In a separate beaker, measure Manutex or similar sodium alginate. Use 10 gm for pouring dyes, 15 gm for painting dyes or 20 gm for screen printing.
3. Add 10 ml of methylated spirit then some of the cooled urea solution and **stir very fast** for a few seconds before pouring it all into the urea solution. Remove any lumps.
4. Add 2 ml of the wetting agent or leveller.
5. Make up to 1 litre with cold water and leave it to stand for 30 minutes. Strain through a sieve, if necessary, to remove any lumps.
6. Before using, add the acid which is necessary for animal fibres, silk and nylon. The pH should be 5.0–5.5. For acetic acid at 30% strength, use approximately 5–6 ml. (I use 10 ml for blues and violets.) For 96% strength glacial acid, 2 ml gives a pH of 5, and 3 ml gives a pH level of 4.5 for the blues, violets, and Cibacrolans.

Using a padding mixture

Presoak the scoured fibre in warm water to which a drop of liquid detergent has been added for 20 minutes. Prepare your table with layers of newspaper, a waterproof layer, then old sheeting or towels to absorb excess dye.

Pour the padding mixture into small beakers and into this add the dye powder or dye solution, and stir it well.

Apply the dyes by your chosen method, leaving clear areas into which the dye may 'bleed' if necessary. When completed, press the dyes into the fibre with the hands or with a rolling pin.

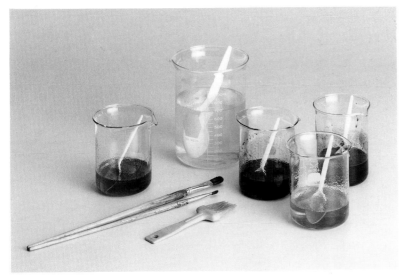

Pour the padding mixture into small beakers and add the dye powder or dye solution and stir it well.

Batch ageing

Remove any towels after dyeing. Roll the fibre into polythene or plastic so that layers of dyed fibre do not touch each other, and seal the edges to exclude air. The time needed to age the dyes depends upon the temperature of the room. In summer 24 hours is sufficient, but in a cold winter climate 48 hours is wiser. Strong shades using more dye are best left for 48 hours. The dye fixation time may be hastened by placing the fibres in a warm situation such as a sunny spot or an airing cupboard, or you may also steam the batches. I usually reserve the latter method for dyes that I have found difficult to fix, and I steam them as a precaution after batch ageing.

Rinsing baths at the conclusion of batching

When it is time to wash out the padding mixture, the rinsing baths contain a little ammonia, which is alkaline and helps to remove any excess dye, and detergent, to assist with the removal of the thickener. The temperature of the rinsing baths is increased or decreased very gradually to avoid any temperature shocks that could cause felting. All cold water dyes should be washed out in this manner whether they have thickener or not.

First rinse: Use cold water to which a little cloudy ammonia is added to give a pH reading of 7.5–8. This will be approximately half a tablespoon to a bucket of water. Merely push the fibre below the surface of the water and leave it to soak for 10 minutes.

Second rinse: The same as for bath 1, but this time add a little liquid detergent. Leave for 10 minutes.

Third rinse: Warm water 45°C (112°F) with a squirt of detergent and half the amount of ammonia. Move the fibre very gently through the water for 10 minutes.

Fourth rinse: Warm-to-hot water 65–70°C (150–158°F) with no ammonia or detergent. Add sufficient acetic acid to neutralize the water to pH 6.5–7. Leave the fibre for 10 minutes.

Fifth rinse: Warm water 30°C (86°F) with no additives. Leave the fibre for five minutes. Squeeze out excess water and dry the fibre away from direct sunlight.

Now wash those polythene sheets and hang them out to dry! If they are large enough, it may be easier to use a hose pipe.

PROCION MX

A recipe for using this cold fibre reactive dye as a dyebath may be found in Chapter Four on p.67. The dye may also be used for direct application. If a thickener is required, the recipe for 1 litre of padding mixture (p.101) may be used, following stages 1–6, except that the 2 ml of wetting agent mentioned in step 4 is replaced with 10 ml of wetting agent Teric.

Just before using the mixture add sodium bisulphite:

For light shades use:	5 gm (1 tsp)
For medium shades use:	10 gm (2 tsp)
For dark shades use:	15 gm (3 tsp)

Pasted dyes can be added to this solution or poured into small beakers and the padding mixture added to them.

The fibre is batch aged for 24–48 hours.

PANFIX W

These dyes are used in the same manner as the Procion MX except that 3 gm (1 tsp) of citric acid is used instead of the acetic acid, and 2 ml Scourbrite leveller replaces the 10 ml of Teric.

Panfix W has a very fast reaction time of 6–12 hours when batch aged in polythene at room temperature, and this may be increased by placing the dyed fibre in a plastic oven bag or foil and baking it in an oven temperature 80°C (176°F) for 15 minutes.

EARTH PALETTE FIBRE REACTIVE DYES

These cold water dyes have all of the necessary chemicals already incorporated into the dye and may be used in any method of direct application. They may be thickened with Manutex if required. Fixing agent A may be added when dyeing greasy unscoured fibres, so that some grease may be retained in the fibre if required.

The fibre is batch aged for 24 hours at a temperature of 20–25°C (68–75°F).

DIRECT APPLICATION ON CELLULOSE FIBRES

FIBRE REACTIVE DYES

Fibre reactive dyes are the easiest to use for direct application methods. Two separate solutions are mixed in advance, and may be stored for many months ready for use. The first is called 'chemical water' and contains urea, water softener (if used) and resist salt (if used). The second solution is the fixative and contains the alkali. When these two solutions are mixed in the presence of dye the reaction takes place.

Resist salts
Some recipes use resist salts such as Resist Salt L (Matexil PAL), Sitol, Ludigol, and Nacon – all trade names for a chemical which prevents the decomposition of the dye while fixing takes place, so giving maximum colour yield. Each name is applicable to a particular dye. For example, Procion MX uses Resist Salt L. Although their use is advisable, it is not essential.

Water softeners
If your water is hard, the impurities affect the dye results and it will be wise to use the water softener sodium hexame taphosphate, which is available at a chemist or drug store. To each litre of water add 0.5 gm of softener. I recommend that you use this chemical in its pure form because proprietary brands may have bleach added which makes them unsuitable for use with dyes.

Stock paste
When block printing or screen printing the dyes need to be thickened with a **stock paste** containing sodium alginate in the form of Manutex or Polycell (p.107). The stock paste contains all the necessary chemical additives.

Fixing
After the fabrics have been dyed, the dyes must be fixed by one of the following methods. See individual recipes for more detailed instructions.

Steaming: Place the fabric or fibre on a sheet of clean plain newsprint, paper towels or clean towelling and roll it up loosely so that no portion touches another. If it is large, the roll may be coiled then tied together. Place this on newspaper on a tray in a steamer, above boiling water. Cover it with a tent made of tin foil to deflect condensation. Steam for 15 minutes.

Oven baking: Prepare the fibre in the same manner as for steaming. Place a bowl of boiling water at the bottom of the oven and place a tray at the top of the oven to baffle the heat from the top element. Place the fibre in a dish mid oven and bake for 10 minutes at 140°C (285°F). Make sure that it does not dry out.

Batch ageing: Place the dyed fibre on polythene and cover it with another layer of polythene or plastic. Seal the edges to exclude the air and allow fixation for the recommended time.

Dyed fabric coiled in newsprint and clean cloth ready for steaming.

Preparations for batch ageing. The dyed fabric is placed on polythene and covered with another layer, before being left to age.

Ironing: Steam iron the fabric for 5 minutes, on the setting recommended for the fibre. Be sure to iron all the dyed areas. Only suitable for small pieces.

Laundry dryer heating: Dry fibre for 20 minutes in a hot cycle of a laundry drier. This is not suitable for silk, rayon, or protein fibres.

Sodium silicate: Water soluble dyes can be mixed with water, painted on to silk then air dried. Purchase sodium silicate from ceramic suppliers. Paint it over the dried surface and leave it to fix for two hours under polythene. Rinse first in cold water then increase temperature to hand hot.

When dyeing cellulose fibres this dye uses Resist Salt L and sodium carbonate (wash soda) or sodium bicarbonate (baking soda) as the alkali to trigger the reaction of dye/fibre bond.

Chemical water
To make 1 litre use: 120 gm urea (10 tbsp) (for rayon use 15 tbsp)
                                            5 gm water softener (1 tsp)
                                            10 gm Resist Salt L (2 tsp)

   Dissolve these in 500 ml (2 cups) hot water, then make up to 1 litre (1 quart) with cold water.

Fixative solution
To make 250 ml (1 cup) use: 1 tsp common salt (sodium chloride)
                                     4 tsp wash soda (sodium carbonate)

   Dissolve in warm water and make up to 250 ml (1 cup) with water.

Dyeing
When you are ready to start dyeing, mix 4 parts of chemical water to 1 part of fixative solution in a beaker, jug or similar container. Use this to paste the dyes and make the dyes to the required strength with this solution. Use the mixed dyes within two hours for maximum colour.

Method 1
This is a reliable method in which the dye is mixed with the chemical water, and the soda is added to start the reaction immediately before dyeing begins. Add the dye to the chemical water.

To 1 litre add: 3g (1 tsp) for pale shades
                                       12 gm (4 tsp) for medium shades
                                       25 gm (8 tsp) for dark shades

   Paste the dye with small amounts of chemical water and mix until completely dissolved. Heat this if necessary. Add this to the remainder of the chemical water. Just before using, mix this fixer:

                                       20 gm (4 tsp) baking soda
                                       5 gm (1 tsp) wash soda or soda ash

   Dissolve the sodas in **hot** water then add to the dye plus chemical water.

Smaller volumes of dye
The recipe for 1 litre may be far too much for your project, so the following makes 1 cup of dye. Mix the ingredients in the same manner as the previous recipe.
   Take 1 cup (250 ml) of chemical water and add the dye.

| *Use:* | 0.75 gm ($\frac{1}{4}$ tsp) for pale shades |
| | 6 gm (2 tsp) for strong shades |

| *Add dissolved alkalis:* | 5 gm (1 tsp) baking soda |
| | 1 gm ($\frac{1}{4}$ tsp) wash soda or soda ash |

Method 2

Soak the fabric for 10 minutes in a solution of 30 gm soda dissolved into 1 litre of water then allow the fabric, which is impregnated with the soda, to dry completely. The dyes can be pasted with a little cold water, then mixed with a chemical water of 5 gm urea dissolved into 100 ml water. The dye may then be directly applied to the dry fabric. Batch age in polythene for 24 hours, or air dry for 12 hours in a warm position, or steam to heat fix the dyes.

Stock paste to thicken dyes for block printing

1. Into 1 litre (1 quart) of chemical water, sprinkle and whisk in:

> 18 gm (4 tsp) Manutex (or similar)
> 10 gm Resist Salt L (or similar)

2. Shake stir or blend, very well. Remove any lumps, and leave to stand for a minimum of 30 minutes.
3. Pour the paste into individual containers and add the dye powder to make dye pastes. There is no alkali in the paste at this stage, so there will be no reaction or fixing if you forget to put it in.
4. For each cup (250 ml) of paste dissolve 5 gm (1 tsp) of bicarbonate of soda in the smallest possible amount of warm water.
5. Just before using the paste add the bicarbonate of soda. The useful life of the dye paste will now be 2 hours.

An alternate method is to mix the dyes with the solutions of chemical water and fixer solutions as described previously, and then to thicken the resulting dye solution with the stock paste. The additional liquid may weaken the dyes, in which case adjust the amount of dye powder accordingly.

Use one of the fixing methods recommended on p.104.

Print pastes for screen printing

The recipe for this paste is thicker than the previous one. To make the thickener:

1. Dissolve 10 gm water softener, if needed, in a small amount of hot water, and add cold water to make up to 1 litre. Sprinkle 50 gm Manutex or similar into this solution, stirring or whisking really well until completely dissolved. Use an electric blender if you prefer. Stand for 30 minutes, until this is clear, and then remove any lumps.
2. A solution is made up of dye + urea + resist salt. In a container or vessel measure:

> 100 gm urea
> 10 gm resist salt

Add 280 ml hot water and stir well until dissolved.
Sprinkle 5–20 gm dye powder, depending upon the required shade, on to the mixture and stir well.

3. Into a container large enough to hold 1 litre, pour 565 ml or grams (just over $^1/_2$ litre or 1 pint) of the thickened paste from stage 1, and pour the dye + urea solution from stage 2 into it. Stir again.

4. Before printing add the alkali:

> 25 gm bicarbonate of soda for cotton
> 12 gm bicarbonate of soda for silk

Dissolve the soda in a small amount of hot water before adding it to the stock paste. The useful life of the paste is now 2 hours.

5. Fix by steaming or oven baking.

PROCION H AND PROCION HE

These dyes are used in the same manner as Procion MX. They will, however, have a longer active life once mixed with the chemical water.

Procion H Black uses wash soda or soda ash instead of baking soda, used in the same proportion. It also requires a reduction of urea in the chemical water. Use 50 gm of urea to each litre of water for this black dye.

When using these dyes for batik work, triple the amount of baking soda recommended for Procion MX dyes. Dry the fabric before ironing out the wax with a dry iron. (This is to prevent a spotting on the dyes by the spots of steam.) Once dry ironed, the fabrics can be steamed in the usual way for 5 minutes, or steam ironed for 10 minutes, or oven baked for 45 minutes at 145°C (300°F).

Print pastes

Procion H/HE dyes may be used for printing in the same manner as Procion MX dyes, providing that the proportion of baking soda added just before dyeing begins is changed to 15 gm (3 tsp) to 250 ml (1 cup) of dye liquid. The fabric will need to be steam set to reach the required fixation temperature.

CIBACRON F

Cibacron F uses Glauber's salt (sodium sulphate) as the alkali and wetting agent Albegal FFD. For best results the liquid temperature when using these dyes should be 20–30°C (70–80°F).

Method

1. To make 1 litre of chemical water use:

> 50 gm urea for pale shades – 100 gm for med/dark shades
> 10 gm Glauber's salt for pale shades – 50 gm for med/dark

Dissolve in 500 ml (2 cups) of hot water then make up to 1 litre with cold water. Add 0.2–0.5 ml Albegal FFD.

2. Add the soda ash, or wash soda, just before using.

For pale shades use: 10 gm of soda
For pale/medium shades use: 15 gm of soda
For med/dark shades use: 20 gm of soda
For dark shades use: 25 gm of soda
For very dark shades use: 30 gm of soda

Dissolve the soda in a minimum of hot water and pour this into the chemical water.

3. Add the dye powder either by sprinkling it on top of the mixture and stirring rapidly, or by pasting it first in a small amount of cold water and then adding it. Alternatively the padding mixture could be poured into smaller pots to which different dye colours are added. Use immediately. Temperature of the mixture should be 20–30°C (70–80°F).

4. Batch age by placing between sheets of polythene to exclude all air. Leave in a comfortable room temperature for 24 hours for light to medium shades and 48 hours for dark shades, or on very cold days. Fix by heat steaming if you prefer this to batch ageing.

5. Rinsing
   a. Overflow in cold water for 2 minutes.
   b. Wash in boiling water for 2 minutes.
   c. Wash in hot water to which detergent has been added, then warm rinse for 2 minutes.
   d. Conclude with a 2 minute rinse in cold water.

These dyes may be thickened with sodium alginate if required for block or screen printing using the Procion MX recipes but omitting the resist salt. When dyeing dark shades increase the amount of soda in the stock paste recipe to 7g (1½ tsp) to each cup of dye paste.

DRIMALAN F AND DRIMARINE K

These dyes use sodium bicarbonate as the alkali (for best results) and resist salt Revatol S.

Method

1. *To make 1 litre of chemical water use:*

50 gm of urea for pale shades
100 gm of urea for med/dark shades

Dissolve this in 500 ml (2 cups) hot water, then make up to 1 litre with cold water. Add 2 ml of Sandozin AMP paste as a wetting agent or substitute with 2 ml liquid detergent.

2. Add the alkali just before using.

For pale shades use: 10 gm of sodium bicarbonate (baking soda)
For med/dark shades use: 20 gm of sodium bicarbonate

Dissolve the soda in a minimum of **hot** water and pour it into the chemical water.
3. Add the dye powder and stir very well until dissolved. The temperature of this padding mixture at the time of use should be a warm 20–30°C (70–80°F).
4. Batch age at room temperature (20–25°C, 70–75°F) for 24 hours.
   Steam fix if you prefer this method to batch ageing.
5. Rinsing. Begin with an overflow rinse in cold water and then wash in hot water (30–40°C, 85–100°F) to which a liquid detergent has been added. Conclude with a cold rinse.

Alternate recipe
The fabric may be pre-soaked in an alkaline solution using 50 gm of soda ash or wash soda to each litre of water. The fabric is then drip dried in air until it is quite dry.

The dye is mixed with the chemical water and can be applied directly to the fabric. Continue fixation and rinsing as in the previous recipe.

Printing pastes
1. Dissolve 10 gm water softener, if needed, in a small amount of hot water and add cold water to make up to 1 litre. Sprinkle 50 gm Manutex or similar into this solution, stirring or whisking really well until completely dissolved. Use an electric blender if you prefer. Allow to stand for 30 minutes, until clear, and then remove any lumps.
2. Another solution is made up of dye + urea + resist salt + alkali.

100 gm urea*
10 gm salt Revatol S (if used)
10 gm sodium bicarbonate**

Add 280 ml of hot water and stir until completely dissolved.
3. Sprinkle the dye powder into this mixture and stir well. The dye powder may also be pasted in cold water before adding to the mixture.
4. Into a container large enough to hold 1 litre, pour the chemical mixture and add the thickener.

* If fixing by steaming (10 minutes at 102°C, 214°F), reduce the amount of urea to 50–80 gm per litre of solution. This will not be necessary if you batch age for 24 hours.
** Sandoz notes that Drimarine Turquoise R–BL must be printed without alkali.

OTHER DYE CLASSES

Other dyes can be used for direct application methods as well as fibre reactive dyes – for instance Sulphur Black (see p.87), Indigosol soluble vat dyes (see p.90) and napthol dyes (see p.91). Some, such as Inkodye vat dye, come mixed ready for immediate use.

INKODYE VAT DYE

This vat dye is premixed to the soluble white or leuco stage and comes in liquid form, ready to use straight from the bottle. It is easy to use for direct application methods such as painting, spongeing and screen printing. The permanent colours may be washed, drycleaned and even bleached, but they are only moderately fast to strong sunlight.

Inkodye is sensitive to light, not air, and exposure to sunlight or daylight is sufficient to return the dye back to an insoluble form. Final colours are not seen until exposed to light so it is therefore necessary to test the colours on small samples before dyeing a major piece. You can use a hot iron to develop colours immediately on small test pieces.

Inkodyes are thinned with water and thickened with sodium alginate.

Mix the colours in the same way as you mix paint. Inkodye Clear may be purchased to mix the dyes to produce pastel shades. Use up to 10 parts Clear to 1 part of dye. To darken the colours, mix with a complementary colour.

After the dyes have been applied, and whilst the fabric is still damp, expose it to sunlight for 90 minutes to develop the dye. If the day is dull or cloudy, increase the exposure time.

Heat fixing is required to set the dyes finally. Steam iron on a cotton setting, or oven bake 130°C (280°F) for 5–15 minutes.

Rinse in warm water, wash in hot water to which a liquid detergent has been added, then rinse in warm water.

Inkodyes may be stored in a cool dark place for up to two years, providing that they are in opaque or dark bottles.

RESIN PIGMENTS

Resin pigments, such as Heatset and Fastex, are not true dyes because the colour sits on the surface of the fabric. They come in the form of a paste which is suitable for screen printing or painting directly onto the fabric. When the fabric is dry the colours are fixed with heat, usually by ironing. The pigments are fast to moderate washing but are not suitable for dry cleaning.

7. CREATIVE DYEING TECHNIQUES

NOVELTY EFFECTS WITH HOT EXHAUST DYEING

Novelties are mainly random, non repeatable, and fun! You do not have to resort to cold pad batch mixtures to achieve novelty effects with dyeing, because there are several ways of using the hot exhaust method to produce random dyeing. If you remember that the dyes need heat, acid for animal fibres and alkali for cellulose, and moisture in which the dye bond may take place, you are free to 'invent' a new dye technique. Reference to the relevant sections on dye classes will help you to work out which additives you need and the fixation time for your dye.

Natural dyes may be used for novelty dyeing. Successful techniques include space dyeing, dip dyeing, knot and tie dyes (see below). Mordants may be used in space dyeing, with several mordants to a hank producing a variety of shades from one dye. You may like to try mordanting a bound skein, removing the binding and then dyeing, to produce two shades. Extend this idea and re-tie a part that has been dyed, and overdye the original colour.

A spinner of handspun yarns has the potential to produce even more intriguing yarns, since the colour of the original fibre affects the dye colour. Brown, black, grey and natural fleeces may be mixed, or a combination of fibres such as angora, silk, or camel, will take the dye to differing degrees. Overdyeing darker fibres produces really subtle shades.

Fibres pre-dyed different colours may be blended together before spinning. Single yarns may be dyed either one colour or random colours, then plied together. Knot yarns look splendid when plied from two different shades. Slubs, spirals, tufts and inserts can be any colour of the rainbow. Dyed fibre may be spun around a core of fine thread, and the single plied in a spiral fashion around another fine yarn, maybe of a different colour. There are endless possibilities (see illustration, p.145).

The following techniques are described for dyeing wool, but the methods can be readily adapted to other fibres. Likewise, those techniques described for cellulose dyes may be adapted for protein fibres.

Space Dyeing

Space dyeing is an extension of hot exhaust dyeing. Prepare a hank of yarn for dyeing. It should be scoured, loosely tied in several places, and soaked in warm water for 20 minutes. Suspend the hank in some manner so that only a portion of it dips into the dyepot. Dye this in the usual manner, then rinse well. Turn the hank and dye another portion a different colour. This may be repeated as many times as you like. I try to plan the position of the dye colours so that a very dark shade does not lie beside a very pale shade, because the distance in value may be discordant in the final product.

Dip dyeing

Dip dyes are prepared in the same manner of suspending a hank so that only a portion of it falls into the dyepot. Pour warm water, to which the acetic acid and the leveller has been added, down the hank and into the empty dye pot. Now put

Space dyeing a skein of yarn.

the dye solution into the dye pot and stir it well. The portion of the hank in the dye pot will dye, and some of the dye will creep up the wet hank. If the hank dries out too soon above the level of the dye bath, the dye may be encouraged to move up the hank with the addition of more water and acid. You may prefer to pour the dye + acetic + leveller, down the hank. When the dye bath is exhausted, the hank may be dropped into it to continue fixation time.

Random effects with dry dye powder

Random rainbow effects, using dry dye powder and steam to fix the dyes, can be most exciting – or a great disaster! You may dye raw fibre, roving, hanks, or pre-wound balls of yarn.

Place the washed and fully dried fibre into a dye pot. Mix warm water, acetic acid and leveller and pour it over the fibre to cover only one third of its depth. Sprinkle small amounts of dye powder on to the top layer. Try a variety of colours but consider the end result when they combine.

Bring the dye bath very slowly to boiling point and simmer for 30 minutes. Check it frequently to make sure that it does not dry out. If you have too much liquid it will boil over the top of the fibre and all the dye powder will mix together before fixing to the fibre. Too much dye powder may also cause the dyes to mix too freely. Leave some patches into which the dyes can migrate.

You may cover the dye to allow steam to form condensation, which will push the dye powder more rapidly into the fibre.

Tie dyeing

Tie dyes and knot dyes are very easy resists. Simply tie a knot in your hank or fibre to act as a resist and dye it in the usual manner. Or you can bind areas that

A pre-wound ball of yarn with dry dye powder sprinkled on top for random rainbow effects. I could microwave this one (see p.145).

A skein of yarn bound with string to resist the dye.

you do not wish the dye to penetrate with a cellulose fibre such as white string or raffia. Cotton twine is excellent for wool dyeing and I feel more confident if I place a small piece of polythene under the binding. Polythene alone is not satisfactory because it allows dyes to slowly penetrate into the fibre.

Injection dyeing

Injection dyes need an eye dropper or something similar to squirt the dye into the fibre, just as it reaches boiling point.

Squirting dye into hot wet yarn pre-wound into a ball.

Into the dye bath put the water and the acetic acid and drop a pre-wound ball of yarn into the bath. Increase the temperature until it reaches boiling. Wearing rubber gloves, remove the fibre, squeeze out the excess liquid, and squirt the dyes into all parts of it. Work fast to keep it warm. Leave some clear patches into which the dye can 'bleed'. Plunge the fibre back into the boiling bath, and hold it below the surface. Simmer for 30 minutes then allow to cool and rinse well.

Painting, spraying and dribbling
Here the oven is used to produce steam for fixing the dyes on painted or sprayed fibre. Soak the yarn, fleece, roving, or fabric in warm water to which acetic acid has been added. Arrange the oven by placing a tray between the top element and the container to hold your dyed fibre, then place a dish of hot water at the bottom of the oven so that steam is formed. Heat the oven to 65°C (150°F).

Squeeze dry or spin dry the fibre. Spray, paint, blob or drizzle the dye across the fibre. If you have used a dye solution above 1% strength, add more acetic acid to the dye. Place the fibre in an enamel, stainless steel or glass dish, mid-oven for 30 minutes. Watch it carefully to ensure that it does not dry out. Allow for considerable creeping or 'bleeding' of the dyes as they soak into the fibre. Fine designs are not possible.

DIRECT APPLICATION ON YARN, FIBRES AND FABRICS

The following methods use cold dyes, which may be suspended in a 'pad' if thickening is desired (see p.101). Remember to include any additives required and to follow the recommended fixing methods for your dye.

Spraying, drizzling, squirting

Spray the dye on to your fibre. You will need to use a relatively thin padding mixture or the nozzle may clog. The dye spreads for considerable distances.

An alternative is to pre-paste the fibre with the padding mixture, then drop, drizzle or squirt the dyes across. The fibre could be covered with polythene and the dyes may be pushed and moved to new places, or merged into each other beneath the surface. This is very suitable for silk fabric.

Fibre may be pre-pasted with padding mixture before dry dye powder is sprinkled across.

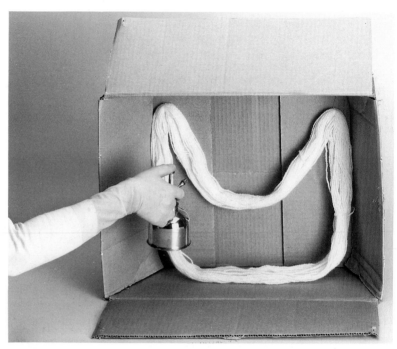

Spray dye on to a hank of yarn suspended in a card–board box to contain the spray.

Prepaste the fibre with the padding mixture then drop dye powder on to the fibre.

Warp painting

The warp may be chained and randomly painted. For precise designs, lie the warp across the length of the table. Make a cardboard or a paper cartoon and stick it to the polythene beside the warp. Keep the warp chained in a bucket on the floor and gradually unchain it. Paint it on the table, then roll it as you progress. Remove any old sheeting that has been used to absorb the excess dye before rolling the warp into the polythene for fixing.

Individual threads may be painted by wrapping them around a plastic pipe or a sheet of perspex.

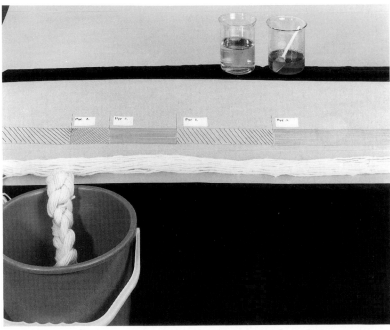

The warp may be chained and painted randomly, or to a pattern. A cartoon fixed above the fibre helps you to follow your design accurately.

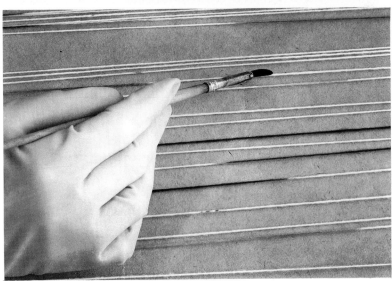

Paint individual threads. In this photograph they are wound around a sheet of perspex.

Pour the dye down a
suspended hank of yarn.

Pouring dye
Pour the dye over unspun fibre, or suspend hanks or rovings of yarn and pour the dyes down them.

Painting a design on fabric
Prepare the design on a cartoon and have it beside you as you work. Have all the dyes mixed before you start. For small areas I use a pastry brush to push the dye into the fibre. Make sure that it has come through to the other side. Fine definition is not possible with this method, so work in larger areas of colour.

Knitted or woven fabrics may be painted without using padding mixture, providing that the correct pH level has been observed and that the fabrics are batch aged for the required time. Rinsing out excess dyes is easier without the thickener.

CREATIVE DYEING ON CELLULOSE FABRICS

Screen printing
Cellulose fabrics (such as cotton T shirts) are very suitable for screen printing, using a thick padding mixture (see Chapter Six).

Some screen printing methods paint the dyes mixed with water directly on to the screen before leaving to dry. The screens are made from a synthetic material which do not react with the dyes. A thickened solution of chemical water stock paste is then forced through the screen to transfer the image from screen to fabric.

Spray dyeing
Spray dye a T shirt with a solution of dye, chemical water and alkali solution, then use one of the fixation methods to establish the dye. You can also make stencils to paint or spray around.

Make stencils to paint or spray around.

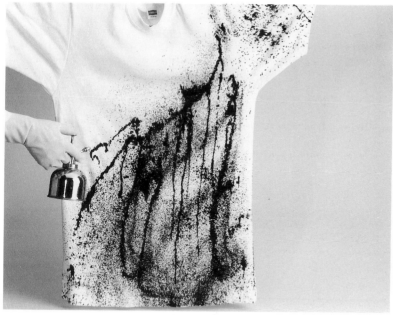

Spray dye a T shirt with a solution of dye, chemical water and alkali solution, then use one of the fixative methods to establish the dye.

Resist dyeing

As the name suggests, resist dyeing introduces a knot, binding or object to prevent the dye taking up in particular areas of the fabric. The photographs on the following pages depict various resist dyeing techniques.

Japanese shibori, and **Malaysian plangi** and **tritik** are sophisticated methods of resist dyeing.

A knotted fabric with rubber bands and soft cotton cord resists.

Screw the fabric into a ball and tie it into a piece of muslin or net curtaining, using rubber bands as a resist for a marbled effect.

To make tiny spots of colour, such as the one in the centre, use a small pin to hold the tip and bind a fine thread beneath the pin and leave it in place during dyeing. The other pins have been used to gather the fabric instead of using stitching.

Linen thread has been bound around buttons of varying sizes, and long beads have been bound with string. Stones could also have been tied into cloth.

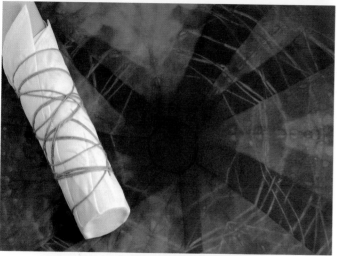

Fold or pleat the fabric around a pole or other type of cylinder, and bind it before dyeing.

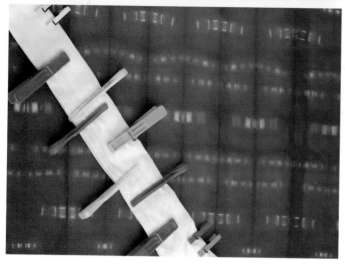

Clothes pegs of differing sizes used as a resist on folded fabric.

Detail from a Javanese textile dyed with indigo, with a batik design of stick puppets. *Otago Museum, Dunedin.*

Japanese everyday cotton kimono for summer wear, showing kasuri method of resisting the dyes in both the warp and the weft. The obi around the waist is cotton with a silk weft with some tiny spots of kasuri in the yarn.

Detail of a Japanese purse showing shibori techniques. The surface has been stitched and bound in small segments to resist the dyes.

Japanese kasuri purse. The warp and weft have been tied in segments to resist the dye in order to produce the pattern. When the dyeing is completed the warp is put on to the loom and weaving begins using the pre-dyed weft. The purse is shown on handmade flax paper dyed with walnut shells.

Use a strong double cotton thread or a single linen thread with a knot at the beginning of the stitching. With tacking or running stitches 0.5–1 cm (^{1}/4–^{1}/2 in) long, stitch a single, double or triple line and pull the threads to gather the fabric. Knot or fasten the end securely. For wider bands, fold the fabric and over sew a seam, gathering it as you progress, then knot or tie off the thread before dyeing.

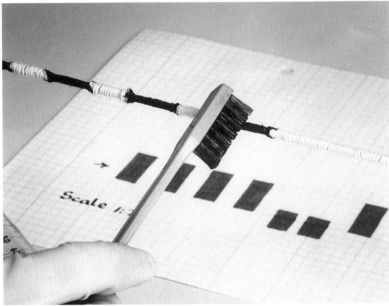

Kasuri or ikat technique.

Kasuri or ikat techniques

These are methods of painting dye between resist bindings on warp and weft yarns which are woven after dyeing is completed and the resist bindings are removed.

Work from a graph or cartoon. Measure and mark the dye areas with tailor's chalk. Bind the resist areas with plastic cooking wrap, and overbind with string. Push the dye into the individual threads with a small stick or a toothbrush. I use fibre reactive dyes which have been thickened with stock paste.

BATIK

Wax has been used for centuries as a resist to dye, usually on silk or cotton fabric. A canting or tjanting is used to draw the hot wax across the fabric. This tool resembles a pen with a reservoir which holds the molten wax and a spout to deliver the wax. If you are unable to purchase a tjanting a brush may be used to apply the wax, but fine definitions will not be possible.

Waxes

Paraffin wax may be used alone but it cracks heavily and is inclined to chip off the fabric. Beeswax is softer, adheres to the fabric well and doesn't crack very much. It is therefore useful to use alone if smooth lines or resist areas are required.

Proportions of wax may be adjusted to suit your needs. A standard wax mixture for batik work uses one part beeswax to two parts paraffin wax.

Heat sources

You will need a heat source near to your work area so that the wax is always hot while you are working. I use tin cans to hold my wax, and place them either in an old saucepan containing water, placed on a gas ring or electric element, or I put the tins of wax in an electric frypan. A double boiler may also be used.

Method

Stretch the fabric across a frame to which it is pinned. Heat the wax until it is liquid and hot. Use the tjanting or brush to apply the wax according to your design.

Look at the back of the fabric to see that the wax has come through to the other side. If not, apply more wax to the underside.

Squeeze the fabric to crackle the cooled wax, if that is part of your design. The dye penetrates to the fabric through the tiny cracks to produce thin lines in a crazed pattern which is most attractive and characteristic of batik work.

An electric frying pan makes a good heat source. A small element is also useful.

A wooden frame keeps the fabric taut and above the work surface. Small pieces may be stretched across a bowl or jar.

Apply the hot wax with a tjanting.

Apply the first dye. The areas covered with wax remain the same colour as the fabric, the clear areas become dyed. Dye baths are the most suitable for all over colour, but direct application by painting, sploshing or dripping are also possible.

When dyeing is completed, the fabric is usually rinsed gently in cold water to remove surplus dye. Dry the fabric and restretch it on the frame.

Rewax areas of the previous waxing if flaking has occurred. Apply more wax to areas you wish to keep the colour of the first dye, then dye the fabric the second

A batik is dropped into a bucket for a long bath dyeing.

colour of your choice. Your second dye will overdye the first (in unwaxed areas) to form a combination of colours. Plan your dye colours before you start dyeing. Dye the lightest colour first, because you cannot overdye a darker colour to make a lighter one. Continue to rewax and redye until you have finished your design.

Wax removal

Crack off loose wax. **Cellulose** fabrics may be boiled in water to remove the wax. Keep an old pot especially for this purpose. Drop the fabric into the pot of boiling water and agitate it for 5 minutes. The molten wax rises to the surface and may be skimmed off. Drop the hot fabric into cold water. Any remaining wax should harden and may be scraped off. If necessary repeat the process, using clean water.

Silk fabrics may be dropped into a pot or bucket containing hot but not boiling water (84°C, 185°F°). Agitate it then remove the silk and drop it into cold water. The surplus wax should fall off. Using fresh water, repeat the hot and cold baths if necessary.

An alternate method for cellulose or silk fabrics

Place the fabric between layers of brown paper, or clean white paper used for newspaper printing, or use paper towels. Iron with a hot iron. As the paper absorbs the wax, remove it and repeat with clean paper.

Cotton may be boiled or washed in soapy water and silk washed in warm water to which a little liquid detergent has been added. Rinse several times in clean, warm water, then dry and press the fabric.

8. PREPARED LIQUID DYES FOR SILK

You will have noticed, when reading previous chapters, that almost all the dyes mentioned are suitable for dyeing silk, either by dipping into a dyebath or by direct application. Those dyes that have been designed for use on animal fibres and require an acidic situation give brighter shades on silk than those for cellulose fibres, which react in an alkaline situation, although both are satisfactory. Silk is damaged by either high temperatures or strong alkalis.

Liquid dyes for direct application on silk are now available. They are highly concentrated and, by using a nozzle, they can be applied straight from the bottle. They are intermixable in eggcups or other small containers, and may be painted onto the silk with a brush or with cotton buds. The dye classes that these dyes fall into are acid, basic or fibre reactive.

The earlier dyes were alcohol based and were in very bright colours. They were fixed by steaming, which some dyers considered to be a messy process. The newer dyes are water soluble, and many have their own brand name of paint-on fixative. The most recently developed dyes combine the fixative with the dye and both are painted on together. What could be simpler than 'paint and wait'? There is also a group of liquid 'dyes' that should be more correctly be called 'paints'. These are applied in the same manner except that the pigments are heat fixed by ironing.

Read the instructions

The trade names of the dyes will differ from country to country. The dye class information is rarely supplied, because it is immaterial, and the instructions supplied with the dyes are all that you really need to know.

Look for three things:
- The method of fixation is obviously most important. You will need to know how long to leave the fixative solution on your silk, or for how long you should steam or iron, if these are the fixation methods.
- Before you use the dyes, you will need to know how to thin them. Some are thinned with water, some with a solution of methylated spirit and water, and some use a supplied fixative.
- Finally, always read the washing instructions to find the wash temperature most suited to the dyes.

Preparation of the silk

The silk is usually prewashed to remove any natural secretions or dirt. Dye has a habit of running into creases and forming puddles, so ironing out any creases will give you a flat surface on which to paint. The silk is then stretched tightly and evenly across a simple wooden frame to which it is pinned.

Cover the sides of the frame with a non-porous sticky tape which can be wiped clean or replaced after use, so that dyes are not absorbed into the wood, only to spoil a subsequent piece of dyeing.

Small pieces may be stretched across a bowl or jar and tied with a soft string, or fixed with an elastic band (see p. 127). Neither the frame nor the silk should touch the table.

WAX AND GUTTA RESISTS

Dyes spread unbelievably rapidly across silk so, for fine definitions, boundary limits are needed to divide different colours or shades from each other. Gutta or wax lines are used as a resist, and are applied with a steady even flow. Check to see that all of the outlines are closed, for any breaks in the gutta or the wax will be found immediately by the migrating dye. Very heavy materials may need to have the resist applied to both sides of the fabric. Dry the resists before you start to paint.

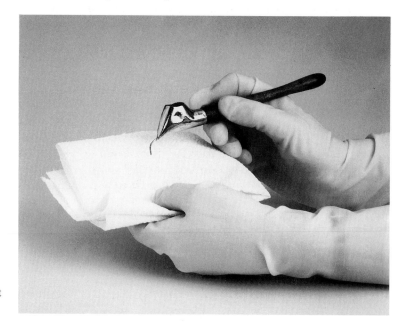

The tjanting is held in this position for application of hot wax to the fabric.

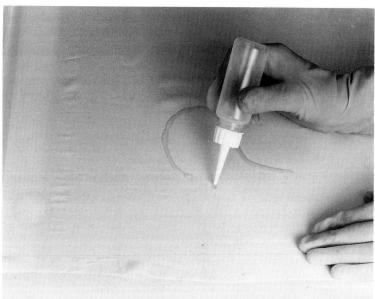

Apply the gutta evenly and smoothly.

Wax

Hot wax can be applied from a brush or, better still, from a tjanting, or canting. The wax stands in a tin which is placed into a pan of hot water to keep it hot. An electric frying pan makes a good heat source, and a small electric element is also very useful.

Hold a paper towel or cloth beneath the tjanting to collect surplus wax when lifting it from the container.

Gutta

Gutta (pronounced 'goota') is a liquid resist used to outline areas which are painted with dye, or to prevent dyes from outside the area penetrating inside. There are two types, both supplied in ready-to-use squeeze bottles. One is **water based**, the other is **spirit based**. The latter dries faster. Clear or white gutta washes out, leaving the silk beneath the original colour. Gold, silver and black outliner however, remains as part of the design.

USING THE DYES

Use cotton buds or a soft brush to apply the dye. For small items, a good quality water colour brush will be ideal. Keep a brush for each colour to save time cleaning or to make sure that dye is not transferred from one colour to another.

Paint the dyes into the centre of an outlined area from where they will run to the resist. If the dye does not reach the outline, apply more dye and press a little more firmly in the centre.

'Watercolour' effects

No gutta, wax or other form of resist is used. Instead the dyes are allowed to run freely into each other. The silk is first wetted, either with water, or with water and thinner combined. Work quickly and freely and be careful not to use too much dye. Watermarks may be made by painting or dropping water, or water and thinner, into areas that have already been painted with dye, and edges may be softened in the same way. This produces a back washing of dye which can be quite attractive. Finer lines or definitions are not so easy to achieve.

The spread of dye has to be halted as quickly as possible. One method is to hold the dye applicator in one hand and a hairdryer in the other and to dry the dye as it touches the silk.

Marbled effects with salt

Salt attracts the water and with it the dye. While the dyes are still damp, scatter salt over all or part of the dyed area, and watch the marbling occur. Try using coarse salt crystals and fine salt particles, because the effects differ. It is of course a basically random effect. The greater the depth of dye colour, the more striking the salt patterns.

Leave the salt on the silk until all is completely dry, then brush it away with a soft brush. The dyes are then fixed according to the manufacturer's instructions.

FIXING METHODS

1. Brush liquid fixatives over the dyed area. Leave it for 1 hour, or the time recommended by the manufacturer.
2. Cover the ironing board with clean cloth. Place the silk on the top, wrong side uppermost, then cover with several sheets of brown paper. Iron at the temperature recommended for 2–3 minutes.
3. Steaming. Roll the cloth into a sheet of absorbent paper such as white newsprint or wallpaper liner. Make sure that the silk is flat with no creases, then roll it into a sausage shape not more than 4 cm ($1^1/2$ ins) in diameter. Seal the edges with tape to exclude air and water.

Liquid fixatives are brushed on with a wide, soft brush, using even strokes. Work horizontally so that they do not run. Make sure you have completely covered the dye.

Place the 'parcel' into a steamer and make a tent out of aluminium foil to put over the silk to pull the condensation away. This 'steamer' contains a cake cooling tray standing on a stainless steel bowl to raise it from the bottom of the pot. There is a little water in the pot to create steam.

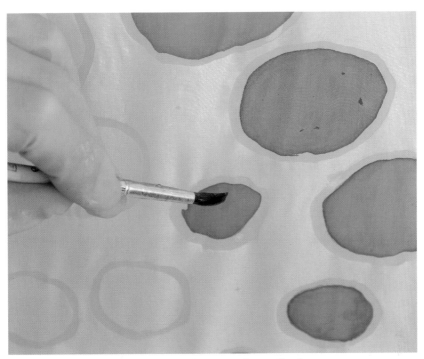

Paint the dyes into the centre of an outlined area.

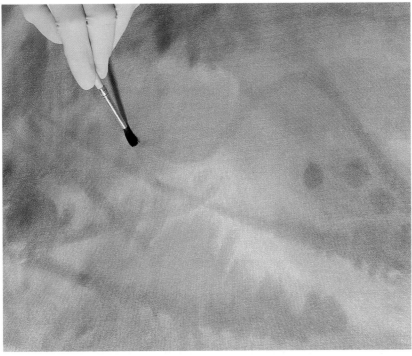

When painting the dyes on to wet silk the colours wash into each other to give a
watercolour effect. Detail of a silk blouse by Diane Harry.

Silk scarf with a marbling effect caused by scattering salt on to wet dyes.

'Falling leaves', a quilted silk jacket by Gyan Bhadra. Hand painted using gold gutta, glitter fabric paint and Deka silk paints. Machine and hand sewn with silk, cotton and gold metallic thread.

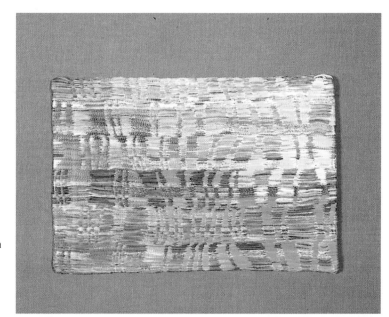

'Water Study'. A wall textile in cotton, rayon and silk by Kelly Thompson. Woven in warp face block weave. The warp was painted with Procion dyes. Size 200mm x 290mm.

Notebook covered in hand-dyed cotton fabric with silver gutta highlight by Diana Parkes.

THE DYES

There are many types of liquid dyes for silk, and new ones are regularly developed. Although the trade name of your dye may differ, it will be similar to one of the dyes described below. Follow the distributor's instructions. If you find you have insufficient detail, write to them for further information.

ELBESOIE

These water soluble **fibre reactive** dyes will dye silk and wool. They are highly concentrated and are diluted with a solution of 50% methylated spirit and 50% water. This solution may be premixed and stored ready for immediate use. The dyes are wash- and lightfast, and also dry cleanable. Fixation is by steaming.

Salt crystals may be used to make marbling effects. You may also try the method of immersing your fibre in a solution of thinned gutta. When it is quite dry, paint the dyes onto the fabric. This should reduce the 'bleeding' of the dyes considerably.

PRINCE OR LEPRINCE

Basic dyes are amongst the earlier forms of synthetic dye, noted for their brilliant, intermixable colours. They dye silk and wool with fair washfast and lightfast qualities. Prince dyes fall into the basic dye category. They are sometimes referred to as 'French silk painting dyes'. The concentrated dyes are in liquid form ready to paint directly onto the fibre.

Princecolor dyes are diluted with water and fixed by steaming, with silk requiring 30 minutes and wool 60 minutes. **Princefix** dyes are diluted with the fixative before application, so that only drying and waiting is required. The minimum dilution is 50/50.

Princecolor and Princefix dyes are available in many colours and may be used with wax or gutta resist or painted like water colours.

ORIENT EXPRESS

This is another **basic** dye and therefore wash- and lightfast qualities are only fair in areas of strong sunlight. The dyes are concentrated, mix well and are diluted with water. The black is very black and the browns are rich shades but the colour chart may not represent the shades well.

Salt may be used to the wet applied dye, prior to drying and fixation. These dyes may also be used for dip dyeing. To a dye bath add two capfuls of dye to each litre of warm water 40°C (100°F). Add 1 tsp of white vinegar and immerse the fibre. Stir gently for 15 minutes and rotate occasionally for 30 minutes.

After the dye has been applied it is left for 48 hours before fixing in a bath. To each litre (quart) add 2 capfuls of fixative, and totally immerse the fibre. Stir it slowly for 5 minutes, then rinse well and dry.

JACQUARD

These are the 'paint and wait' dyes which come in a good range of bright colours. They will dye silk, cotton or wool, though the latter requires much more dye.

The dye is mixed with the fixative at a minimum rate of 50/50, applied to the fabric, and after a waiting period is ready to wash out.

DEKA-SILK, ELBETEX, SOLINE

These are heat set pigments which can be painted on in the same way as the liquid dyes. They have a moderate wash fastness up to 60°C (140°F), good light fastness and are dry cleanable.

The dyes may be painted between gutta or wax, painted directly onto the fabric and backwashed with water to give watercolour effects, or salt may be sprinkled onto the wet dyes to give marbled effects. Deka-silk produces outliners similar to gutta, in gold, silver or colourless liquids. Elbetex produces a water-based gutta.

They are fixed when dry by ironing the fabric on the wrong side for 2–3 minutes with the iron set between silk and wool.

9. DYEING SYNTHETIC FIBRES

DISPERSE DYES

Previously mentioned dyes are not suitable for man-made fibres, with the exception of nylon which responds well to dyes suitable for animal fibres. Disperse dyes were developed for dyeing acetates, and they are suitable for polyester, nylon, orlon, dacron, and many other synthetic fibres.

Brand name	Manufacturer
Celliton	BASF
Resolin	Bayer
Cibacet	Ciba-Geigy
Teraprint	Ciba-Geigy
Terasil	Ciba-Geigy
Samaron	Hoechst
Dispersol	ICI
Duranol	ICI
Solacet	ICI
Artisil	Sandoz
Foron	Sandoz

Disperse dyes may be applied in a dye bath, by direct application or by heat transfer. Disperse dyes do not dissolve in water. They are dispersed throughout the water, and will penetrate the fibre when heated. After direct application, therefore, the fabric will need to be heated by ironing, steaming, or baking. Some print on paper and some, such as fabric crayons, are heat pressed directly on to the fabric. Disperse dyes are moderately wash- and lightfast.

The dyes are concentrated and require a chemical carrier, which is usually sold with the dyes. The carrier must be used with care, in a well ventilated room.

DYE BATH

You will need a stainless steel or enamelled dye pot which is large enough to hold the fibre and to allow good circulation of liquid. Other metals, such as aluminium, tin or galvanized iron are not suitable. This recipe is for 100 gm weight of fibre. The liquor ratio is 30:1. You will need:

Soap flakes: 1 gm per litre of water = 3 gm
Acetic acid ($33^1/3$% strength): 1 ml per 100 gm of fibre (1%) = 1 ml
or white vinegar: 3 ml ($^1/2$ tsp)
Dye powder: 0.5 gm ($^1/2$ tsp) will dye to a medium dark shade.

If the chemical carrier is supplied, it is used in relationship to the weight of the fibre:

Pale shades: 6% weight of fibre (6 ml)
Medium shades: 9% weight of fibre (9 ml)
Dark shades: 12% weight of fibre (12 ml)

Method
1. Prescour the fibre or fabric to remove size, dirt or starch, and thoroughly wet it before immersing into the dye bath.
2. Into the dye pot pour warm water, hand hot, in the region of 55°C (130°F). Add the acetic acid, the soap, and the carrier. Enter the fibre and soak it in the solution for 5–10 minutes.
3. Meanwhile paste the dye with a little cold water. Add sufficient boiling water to completely dissolve the dye. Remove the fibre from the dye bath and add the dye. Stir well before re-entering the fibre.
4. Raise the temperature of the bath to 90–100°C (195–212°F). Simmer just below boiling for 1 hour.
5. Wash the fibre in hot soapy water then given several warm rinses.

DIRECT APPLICATION

When using these dyes for direct application methods (see Chapter Six), the dyes are mixed with a chemical water containing urea and water softener (if needed). This may also be thickened with sodium alginate (Manutex, Polycell or similar) for screen or block printing.

To make 1 litre (1 quart) of chemical water

    140 gm urea
    4 gm water softener
    10 ml wetting agent Ludigol (or substitute dishwashing liquid)

Into a vessel large enough to hold 1 litre (1 quart) of liquid, pour 500 ml (2 cups) of hot water. Add the water softener, urea, and wetting agent, and stir well. Make this up to 1 litre with 500 ml (2 cups) of cold water.

To mix the dyes
Sprinkle between 0.5 gm and 5 gm dye ($^1/2$–5 tsp) (depending on the shade required) on to the chemical water and stir until dissolved. Add to the mixture 15 ml of white vinegar to each 5gm of dye used (1 tbsp for each tsp of dye used).

To make a print paste
The chemical water may be thickened by the addition of sodium alginate. Use 18 gm (4 tsp) for screen printing. Wet the Manutex or Polycell with approximately 10 ml (1 dspn) of methylated spirit, and immediately pour in some of the chemical water. Stir very rapidly then add it all to the main bulk of the chemical water. If you prefer you may mix it with a whisk or blender.

Fixing
Heat fixing is necessary for disperse dyes applied directly. Steam iron for 4–5 minutes, or steam in a vessel for 30 minutes. If you intend using a steamer, reduce the amount of urea by half, to 70 gm (5 tbsp).

   Rinse in cold running water. Follow with a hot wash containing a liquid detergent and conclude with warm rinses.

HEAT TRANSFER

When disperse dyes are heated they become gaseous and the vapour is absorbed by polyesters and acetates. Heat transfer is a method whereby the dyes are applied by painting or screen or block printing on to paper and, when dry, the image is transferred from the paper to the fabric by pressure ironing. Pressure, heat and time are needed to convert the dye from solid to gaseous form. An ironing press is excellent, but a flat iron, preferably without steam holes, will suffice. When pressing, great care must be taken not to scorch the fabric. Layers of brown paper are placed between the iron and the fabric.

A print paste for heat transfer

1. Mix 15 gm dye (1 tbsp) to a smooth paste with 15 ml (1 tbsp) of cold water.
2. Add 250 ml (1 cup) of water that has been thickened with 18 g (4 tsp) sodium alginate.
3. Add 15 ml (1 tbsp) methylated spirit, and stir well. The amount of methylated spirit used relates to the amount of dye. As the dye increases, so does the quantity of methylated spirit.
4. Paint, screen or block print on to smooth non-absorbent paper, or heat transfer paper. Let it dry completely. At this stage it may be stored until needed, providing that it is kept dry.
5. Make a soft bedding on your table, ironing board or press and place the fabric on it. Place the print paper on top of the fabric, printed side down, and cover with layers of brown paper.
6. Press hard for 45–60 seconds, using 'cotton' heat on the iron or press. The image will be reversed when transferred to the fabric.

DYE CRAYONS

Dye crayons work in the same manner. They are fun, and very safe for children to use. In the packet the colours appear dull and uninteresting, but once ironed the brilliant colours develop.

10. DYEING WITH A MICROWAVE OVEN

The microwave oven is an excellent tool for the modern dyer. It is most useful for dyeing small quantities of protein fibre, particularly for test samples. There is little advantage in using it for cellulose fibres.

MICROWAVE OVENS AS A HEAT SOURCE

Microwaves are electromagnetic waves similar to those in radio, light, and heat waves. They are used for transmitting telephone and TV signals – and for cooking.

There is little difference between dyeing in a conventional hot exhaust dye bath and dyeing in a microwave oven. Dye shades are identical, for the oven is merely a heat source. The difference is speed. The water molecules within the dye liquid and fibre vibrate at a rapid rate when they absorb microwave energy. This friction causes heat and the dye liquid becomes hot. A microwave does not damage the fibre unless the dye bath dries up – the fibre will then burn, and the magnatron will be damaged. However, dyeing time in a microwave is so short that it is no hardship to check the moisture level every few minutes. The shorter 'cooking time' means less evaporation of the liquid, and less water is therefore needed.

The microwave oven does not hold large quantities of fibre or liquid, and in fact large volumes of liquid take almost as long to heat as when heated on a conventional heat source.

Use your microwave in the manner prescribed by the manufacturer. If you are using one for the first time, read the instructions before you start.

No metals are used in a microwave oven, and this includes twisty metal ties for securing. Dye baths and utensils will be made of pottery, glass, or microwave-safe plastic, and are kept specifically for dyeing. The size of the dye vessel will be suggested by the amount of fibre that you wish to dye. You may like to consider purchasing an ovenware casserole with a lid, if you intend dyeing regularly in your microwave oven. In the absence of a lid, I cover the dye bath with a saucer or plate.

When using plastic film to cover the dye bath, leave unsealed spaces at the corners so that the steam can escape. Dye liquid often escapes at the same time, so you will need to keep a cloth nearby to mop up any spills. The dyes will cause no damage and will leave no residue to harm food which is subsequently cooked inside the oven.

Fumes from acids are powerful when carried in the steam, so be careful not to inhale them. Care is also needed when removing plastic film, because escaping steam can burn your skin.

DYEING PROCEDURE

Match each stage of dyeing as closely as possible to that of hot exhaust dyeing, with the exception of times. Refer to the relevant section to see how your dye functions best. The fibre or fabric must be well scoured because any residual grease heats in the microwave oven to form 'hot spots'. Pre-soak the fibre in warm water for at least 20 minutes, then when dyeing commences, squeeze it between towels so that it is merely damp.

There will be no colour loss if the following rules are observed:

1. The pH level is correct for the dye that you are using.
2. The temperature for dye fixation has been reached.
3. Fixing time has been included.
4. There is freedom of movement of fibre in the liquid, and the fibre has been rotated regularly to give level results.
5. The correct leveller for the dye has been used. If you are not sure, use a neutral liquid detergent. Too much leveller acts as a resist, and therefore care with reducing the amounts for small samples is necessary. Refer to p.58 .

Most dye recipes state that the dye bath should be started with warm water. When using a microwave oven I use hot water. This saves time and heat. Add the necessary chemicals, enter the damp fibre and allow it to absorb the chemicals for 15–20 minutes. The water should have cooled to hand hot. Remove the fibre and add the dye, then stir well and re-enter the fibre. Push the fibre below the surface of the liquid. You might find that a weight is needed to keep it in this position.

Heat on power 100% until bubbles indicate that boiling point is approaching, and rotate the fibre frequently during this period. The exact amount of time will depend upon the volume of your dye bath and the power of your oven. When you feel that boiling point has been reached, reduce the power to 70–75% and continue to 'cook' for the fixation time. The fibre will only need to be moved once or twice during this time.

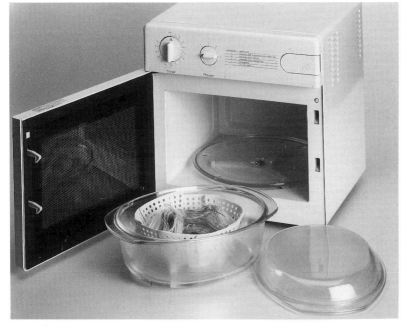

A casserole with a lid and a microwave safe steamer are very useful if you intend to do a lot of dyeing in your microwave oven. Microwave safe plastic cooking bags are an excellent substitute.

Fixation time in a microwave oven is one quarter of the time given for conventional heat sources. Pale shades will need 10 minutes and stronger shades 15 minutes. Thinner areas of fibre mass will heat quicker than dense areas, and dye will therefore bond faster in those areas. Arrange the fibre evenly to ensure a level dye.

Cool the dye bath without removing the fibre. This is standing time and the dye will continue to exhaust. If dye remains in the liquor, the pH level may have been too low and you can try a little more acid and a little more 'cooking time', or the fibre may have already taken as much dye as it is able. If you find that the dyes are not quite as level as you would have liked, it may be that the dyes have taken too quickly and not had time to level. This sometimes happens when dyeing in small volumes of dye liquor, which reach boiling point very fast. Correct this by dyeing on a lower power level, or reducing the temperature of the initial dye liquor.

Strong concentrations of dye may not fix by steaming alone. If using dye above 1% concentration, add more acid to the soaking solution or to the dye solution. At the completion of dyeing and fixing time, the fibre may be placed into hot water and it may be brought once again to boiling point to ensure maximum take up.

Providing that the dyed fibre holds sufficient moisture, it may be 'cooked' without a steamer. Simply place it into a lidded container and continue in the same manner. Small explosions may occur if the fibre becomes too dry. This situation can be prevented by placing a cup half filled with water in the dye vessel with the fibre. Microwave plastic film makes a lid, but needs perforations to allow the steam to escape as heating continues. Watch the moisture level, and add more water if needed.

Tie dyes and knot dyes are just as easy to do in the microwave oven as by the usual hot exhaust method.

NOVELTY DYEING IN THE MICROWAVE

If we presoak the fibre in the chemical additives necessary for the dye/fibre bond, we can squeeze out the excess moisture and place the dye powder or solution exactly where we please, and put it into the microwave oven for a speedy fixation. This is the essence of novelty dyeing. Only clean scoured fibres and fabrics will dye successfully, and any grease left in fleece will heat to cause small explosions.

Random dyes

Soak the fibre in hand hot water to which the leveller and other additives are present. Remove the fibre and squeeze out the excess moisture.

Pour dye solutions across the fibre, or use an eye dropper to place the solutions where you please. If you use too much solution it will 'puddle' in the base of the container and mix to give an overall dye colour.

Place the fibre into some sort of non-metallic steamer inside the dye vessel, which has water in the base to produce the steam. I have a small vegetable steamer designed for the microwave oven, in which I can place the fibre. It sits inside my dye casserole which contains the water to produce the steam. You may be able to design your own from a microwave-safe plastic container.

Cover the dye vessel to retain the steam. Use power level 100% for 5 minutes and turn the fibre if you think it is necessary. Reduce the power to 70–75% and continue to 'cook' for 10 minutes. It is crucial that you watch the moisture content both in the dye vessel and in the fibre. Extra water may be added to either.

Dry dye powder

Instead of using dye solution, you can sprinkle dry dye powder over the fibre. If you use too much it will cause small explosions in the oven. Less dye is used if you shake it through a fine sieve, or a coarse muslin cloth. I have tried putting it on with a small dry brush and this seems to work well too. Steam the dyes in the same manner as when using dye solutions.

Injection dyes

Injection dyes (see p.114) are easier to do in a microwave oven because the hot water continues to boil during standing time and is still at boiling point as you re-enter the balls of yarn. Put the acetic acid into the water, and soak the fibre in it as the water heats to boiling point. No leveller is required because we wish an immediate dye/fibre bond. After entering the dyed fibre, heat on power 100% until bubbles appear, then reduce to power 70–75% for 10 minutes to fix the dye.

Handspun novelty yarns by Ann Milner.

From left to right:
1. Tussah silk, white china silk and lurex thread plied together.
2. Cotton slub plied with space dyed silk yarn.
3. Bouclé yarn using peach and lavender singles, plied again with a white slubby angora.
4. Woollen yarn from four shades of dyed fleece blended together.
5. Dyed fleece core spun onto a fine thread then plied in a spiral manner with another fine thread.
6. One ply of cold pad dyed silk fibre, plied with angora and dyed silk yarn.
7. Tufts of space dyed two-ply yarn, placed between two black singles and knotted individually during plying.
8. Black wool singles and coloured sewing thread plied into a knot yarn.

11. DYEING WOOL FOR FELT

Throughout the previous chapters constant reference has been made to the fact that in a warm, wet situation such as a dye bath, animal fibres will felt when friction is applied. The felter wishes full manipulative control and does not want the felting to take place in the dye bath. If the fibres are already matting together they will be difficult to handle and may lose some character. Previously constructed felt may shrink in the dye bath and this could be a disaster. The rule for dyeing fibre for felting is therefore to avoid friction in the dye bath by moving the fibre very gently through the bath and reducing the boiling to a simmer, so that the bubbles do not cause any friction through the fibre.

Your fibre must be well scoured before dyeing to remove dirt and grease. If you are using pre-carded roving or batts, tie or sew the layers into muslin so that they do not float away in their liquor. Soak the fibre for 30 minutes in warm water to which a little liquid detergent has been added prior to dyeing. When dyeing after felting has been completed, there is obviously no need to scour again, but pre-soaking is recommended for level dyeing.

If you prefer to use natural dyes, you will need to be sure that the colours will not be affected by the alkali in the soap that you will use during the felting process. Most berry dyes will change from purple to green in an alkali. Try a small test piece first.

You will be able to reduce some of the friction in the dye bath by putting the mordant and dyestuff in the bath together. Your dye time must then be at least the 45 minutes needed by the mordant to bond to the fibre.

The chemical dyes most suitable for felting are those with good washfast properties, such as fibre reactives, premetallized 1:2 dyes or those such as Lanaset, which are a mixture of the two. The cold dyes are excellent because friction through heat has been eliminated. Omit the thickeners unless you are screen printing. Use the urea, acid, dye and the recommended levelling agent as described in the cold pad batch method. Some dyes such as Earth Palette have the additives already. Dyes spread a considerable distance across the fibres, but this can be reduced by dyeing the felt whilst still dry.

Some felters dye their fibre first and then card different colours together, or layer different coloured fibre to felt them together. It is possible to cut through the felt to expose the layers of colour. It is also possible to dye the fibre before felting it, and re-dyeing in some manner after the felt has been made.

Suggested fleece types for felting are: Merino, Polworth, New Zealand half bred, Corriedale, Romney and Coopworth. The fibre colour, whether white, cream, grey or black, will affect the ultimate dye colour. Other fibres such as camel wool, mohair and angora may also be used for felt-making. There are plenty of exciting combinations to try.

12. DYES FOR HANDMADE PAPER

Paper-making is a fascinating craft which I shall outline only briefly here. Your public library should have more detailed books on the subject, and I recommend looking for classes at your local night school or craft centre.

Handmade paper may be made from natural plant material or from recycled paper which has been shredded, pulped and reformed. In both forms the fibres are all cellulose and therefore any dye, whether natural or synthetic, that dyes cellulose fibre may be considered suitable for colouring paper.

NATURAL FIBRES

Plant materials suitable for making paper are quite easily available and fun to gather. Most leaves have insufficient fibre, with the exception of lily leaves, banana leaves and agave leaves, but some plant stalks, such as daffodil, potato, and *Protea nerifolia* have sufficient fibre, and sturdy grasses, rushes, nettles and flaxes will all be useful.

The shades and textures of handmade paper from gathered plant sources are so subtle and so beautiful that, personally, I am reluctant to change them in any way. My very small collection includes pale ivory shades from New Zealand grass (*Oryzopsis rigida*), greenish yellow from southern cutty grass (*Carex appressa*), browns from iris leaves, and a wonderful rich purple mahogany from red hot poker (*Kniphofia*).

If you do wish to add a dye colour you will need to take into consideration the original colour of the fibre, for the natural shading becomes part of the dye colour. I have found that only the pale natural fibres will dye successfully.

The process of making paper from natural plant material, very briefly and simply, entails breaking the fibres into small lengths, cooking them in strong alkali solutions of either soda ash (sodium carbonate) or caustic soda (sodium hydroxide) in order to break down and soften the fibre, then washing it to remove the alkali completely. The fibre is then beaten to roughen and separate the strands.

A bath of suspended fibre filaments is made and from this the paper is made by scooping mesh-covered frames into the bath, bringing them to the surface to drain, then transferring the resulting sheet of fibre on to a board or felt cloth ready to be slowly pressed and dried. The fibre may also be left on the screen or frame to dry.

The amount of caustic soda used is 15–20% the weight of the fibre. This is really strong, and the usual precautions of adding the soda to **cold** water should be observed, and masks, rubber gloves, goggles and other protective gear should be worn. Work in a well ventilated room because the fumes can be dangerous, and even more so if you make the mistake of using an aluminium dye pot!

RECYCLED MATERIALS

Using recycled material is much quicker than using natural fibres, because the breaking down of the fibres has already been completed. If you are using

Scooping a sheet of paper from a bath containing suspended plant fibre.

recycled paper that has previously been bleached white, you will find that the dye shades are brighter and clearer than those on natural plant fibre.

The recycled paper should be shredded, and soaked in water before pulping. This stage is also your dye bath stage, with either natural dye plus mordant, if needed, or with synthetic dye plus any necessary chemicals, added to the 'dye bath'. Follow the instructions on how to use the dyes in the relevant chapters. You will need to know the weight of your fibre before you begin, in order to assess the quantity of dye or chemical assistants to use.

Cotton linters for paper making are available in some parts of the world. Dye them as for cotton and then process for paper-making.

DYEING

Any dyes used during the boiling up process must be tolerant of an alkaline situation. I have experimented with adding natural and chemical dyes to the soda and fibre cooking stage, and had either poor or negative results. For the best results, then, I recommend dyeing the fibre after it has been boiled, washed, and beaten. This will mean that the fibre will need to be re-washed after dyeing, and you may need a finer muslin or mesh across your rinsing bath in order to retain the fine beaten fibres.

Natural dyes

Only strong dyes will overdye the natural fibre colour and penetrate the tough cellulose fibres. If you achieve a good strong dye shade on wool, try it on cellulose. You will also be looking for a dye which doesn't fade.

Tree barks and seeds containing tannins give strong browns and green browns. Tanekaha bark (celery leaved pine), and *Coprosma grandifolia* bark give good shades. I have used the potent dye liquor from tanekaha bark (obtained from felled trees) to give a rich red brown colour to paper. I have also used iron or copper sulphate mordants to darken natural dyes, and have been rewarded with some handsome grey, and grey brown shades.

Acorns, walnut shells, and flax roots are also very useful. Soak them for a few days in water to extract maximum colour before dyeing.

Dandelion, gorse, foxglove, chrysanthemum, buddleia, and flax, using alum or chrome mordants on white or cream paper pulp, will give yellow, yellow-green shades

Some lichens will produce good colours, especially the *Parmelia* species (crottles). Usnea or 'old man's beard' may give good shades in your area. Remember that lichens require a two-hour simmer to extract the colour.

All dye materials need to be wrapped in a muslin bag to prevent them from tangling with the fibres, unless you choose them to be an integral part of the finished paper. Alternately extract the dye from the dye material and use only the dye liquor to dye the paper pulp.

The dye shades produced from natural dyes are generally so similar to the natural shadings of plant fibre paper that there is little merit in using these dyes for these fibres, although they may be considered useful for adding an extra depth of colour to a pale paper.

Chemical dyes

Chemical dyes most suitable for paper are those that are simple to use. The most readily available are the household or union dyes purchased from a chemist or local store. The Procion MX-based Dylon dyes will successfully dye the cellulose fibres. Direct dyes such as Deka L have good lightfast qualities, and because paper does not need to be washed, their moderate washfast qualities will not need to be taken into account. If a fixative is supplied, use it in the prescribed manner.

The household and direct dyes are made into a paste then added to the dye bath containing the fibre. The temperature is raised to fix the dye.

The fibre reactive dyes such as Procion MX, and Cibacron F require the alkali soda ash (washing soda/sodium carbonate) to allow the dye to react. Salt (sodium chloride) may be omitted from dyes for paper, because levelling is not important – any slight colour differences in the fibre will be attractive in the final paper. For these dyes I use the longbath method using warm water at 40°C (105°F). Once the fibre and the dye is added, the bath needs to be stirred well to separate the fibres that tend to clump together. After 10 minutes I add the wash soda (10% weight of fibre) and stir every few minutes for an hour. The fibre will need to be washed again to remove all excess dye before making it into paper.

Fibre reactive 'cold' dyes, especially in the G (yellow) range of colours, can be mixed to produce the same shades as natural plant dyes, and save on the cost of expensive mordants.

Recipes for all of these dyes may be found in Chapter Six.

13. COLOUR

Many of you will have an inherent instinct for sound or exciting choices of colour. This chapter endeavours to help those of you who find colour choices more difficult to make. By understanding some basic principles a safe starting place may be found.

Dyes are colouring agents and therefore the pigment theory of colour will be used here. This theory supposes that the primaries are of equal brilliance and are pure colour. In other words, they contain no hint of either of the other primaries – ie, red has no leaning to either yellow or blue. However, dye primaries are rarely pure. Let us look at colour from a dyer's perspective.

When we look at a blue vase, we actually see the blue light waves reflected from the vase. The other colour light waves have been absorbed or subtracted by the vase. This process is called **subtractive**. A black surface absorbs all the colour light waves, and a white surface reflects all colour light waves, subtracting nothing. A dyed fabric or fibre absorbs all of the light waves and reflects those indicated on the dye label.

You will often see references to **hue**. This merely means the name of a colour of the spectrum: blue, green, yellow. The hue red may be orange, pink, maroon or apricot.

PRIMARY AND SECONDARY COLOURS

Red, yellow and blue, are called **primary colours** because they cannot be mixed from any other colours and yet from these primaries all other colours including black, can be mixed.

A **secondary colour** can be mixed from equal amounts of two primary colours.

> blue + yellow = green
> blue + red = violet
> red + yellow = orange

The easiest way to assemble colours to allow us to see the relationship between primary and secondary colours, is within a 'colour wheel'. Colours are arranged in their natural order as they appear in a rainbow. Each wheel contains the three primary colours, and the three secondary colours are placed midway between the two primaries from which they were made.

You can see that yellow relates to orange, and to green, because it is used in the make-up of both colours.

This is the minimum number of segments in a colour wheel, but the most useful number is probably 12. Each primary is mixed in equal amounts with its neighbouring secondary to produce an **intermediate colour.**

> yellow + orange = yellow/orange
> blue + violet = blue/violet

These colours are placed in their natural order within the wheel.

You will notice that hues nearest to yellow give a relative feeling of warmth. They are often referred to as 'warm' colours. Those furthest away, nearer to the violets and blues, generally appear cooler and are referred to as 'cool' colours.

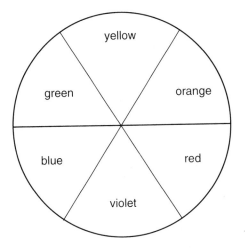

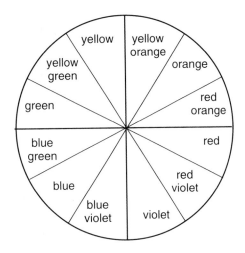

Mixing colours using all primaries

I have drawn a triangle inside the colour wheel linking the three primary hues of red, blue and yellow. If you mix three primaries of equal brilliance and pure colour, in equal proportions, you will make black or dark grey. This appears in the centre of the wheel. The graduated triangle on p.154 relates directly with this diagram.

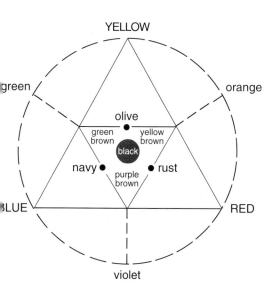

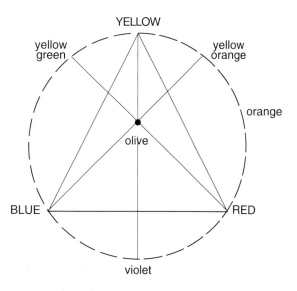

Mix:

green + orange in equal proportions = olive
green + violet in equal proportions = navy
orange + violet in equal proportions = rust

You can approach a colour from any area of the triangle or circle providing that an intersecting line cuts through the colour. For example olive may be mixed by using yellow and violet, yellow and black, blue and yellow/orange, red and yellow/green, yellow and navy, in the correct proportions.

Navy may be mixed from green and violet, blue and orange, red and blue/green, in the correct proportions. If the navy is not as dark as you had anticipated, use more dye, and dye to a greater depth of shade.

By drawing a line through two points within the triangle, you will be able to observe which areas the line passes through, and be able to anticipate what to expect when mixing two colours together.

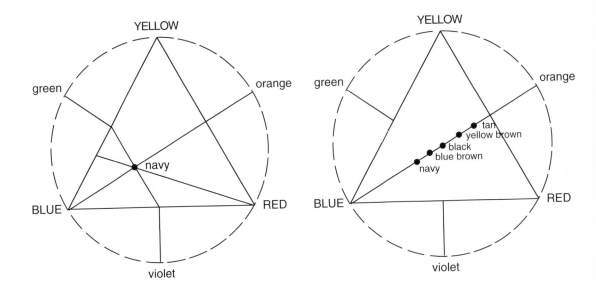

DYE COLOURS

When you choose dyes, no colour is labelled 'pure'. In other words they contain hints of the other two primaries. The red may be labelled Red B, Red 5B, Red G, or Red 3G as we have seen in Chapter Three. When you use paint to mix colours, you will find that the scarlet is similar to Red G, the crimson nearer to Red B. The cobalt is similar to Blue G, and the ultramarine more like Blue R. Yellow ochre is similar to Yellow R.

To obtain the clearest violet, use Red B and Blue R or, with paints, crimson and ultramarine. Neither have a G (yellow) suffix, and therefore the yellow will not get into the mixture and dull the colour. If you mix Red G and Blue G, or scarlet and cobalt, you will see the difference.

MIXING DYE COLOURS

The exact position of navy, rust, olive, or grey within a triangle produced from three primaries will depend upon which dye is used. Yellow 4G has more pure yellow than Yellow 2G, and therefore there will be more yellow shading within the triangle, and the greys will be nearer to the baseline. The colours produced from the mixing of Red G and yellow are quite different from those mixing Red B and the same yellow.

Here are two triangles using three primaries, but using different reds and blues. Both are at the same depth of dye.

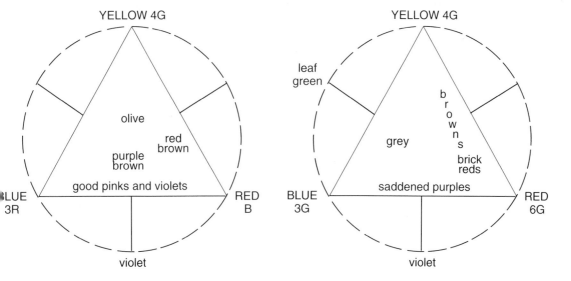

Triangle 1 uses Yellow 4G, Blue 3G and Red 6G. It produces warm shades because each primary has a leaning towards yellow. All of the shades relate because of the G base. Many natural dye shades may be matched on this triangle, especially towards the centre where the shades are muted. There are leafy greens, earthy green/golds, olives, ochres, and chartreuse. The browns are excellent oaks and red/browns. There are brick reds and terracotta. When the depth of shade is reduced to $1/8\%$ or less, the same triangle has peaches, warm pinks, creams, and smoke pinks on the base line. (See illustration, p.157.)

Triangle 2 uses Red B and Blue 3R with Yellow 4G. There is no hint of yellow in either of them and the colours are 'cooler' than on the previous triangle. The purples are clear and exiting. greens are more peacock, and the browns are more walnut. When the depth of shade is reduced to $1/8\%$ or less the triangle shows many clear pinks and lavenders.

Greens from this triangle look best with other shades from the same chart, and sit less comfortably when exchanged and placed into the G (yellow) based range. The same applies to all colours on both triangles. However, as a contrast or highlight to excite the eye, place them in small amounts with colours produced from the other primary grouping.

There are many other primary combinations. For example the blue may be replaced with turquoise, and the red with magenta.

PRACTICAL COLOUR MIXING

Colour mixing trials in some form or other are essential, particularly if you find it difficult to grasp the purely theoretical approach to colour changes and combinations. Using percentage mixing methods you can make two-colour value change charts and colour triangles to provide a visual reference and a practical demonstration of the theories outlined above. You will soon see the benefit of making them if you want to find which dye combinations produce walnut browns or golden oaks, for example.

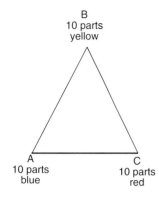

B
10 parts
yellow

A
10 parts
blue

C
10 parts
red

A graduated colour triangle using three hues

A trichromatic triangle, using three primary colours, not only shows the secondary shades where two are mixed (on the outside of the triangle), but also contains the subtle tertiary colours from the mixing of the three dyes in the centre of the triangle.

The squares are numbered 1 to 66 for ease of identification. Each dye square in the triangle is divided into 10 parts. The topmost square in this example (square 1) is completely yellow and all 10 parts are yellow; no parts are either red or blue. As we progress down into the row below, the yellow is reduced to 9 parts. The left side of the triangle is going to gradually increase the blue content down to the base – square 56 which will be all blue. The red content will increase on the right side and down to the final square 66, which will have all 10 parts red.

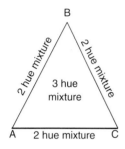

B

2 hue mixture

2 hue mixture

3 hue
mixture

A   2 hue mixture   C

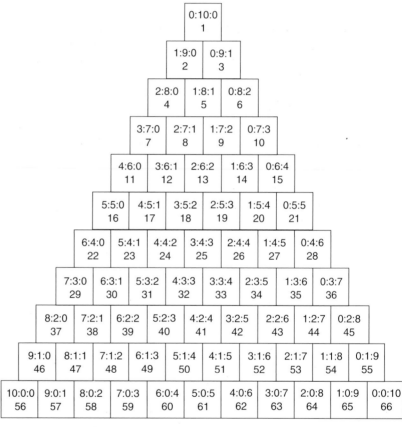

						0:10:0 1					
					1:9:0 2		0:9:1 3				
				2:8:0 4		1:8:1 5		0:8:2 6			
			3:7:0 7		2:7:1 8		1:7:2 9		0:7:3 10		
		4:6:0 11		3:6:1 12		2:6:2 13		1:6:3 14		0:6:4 15	
	5:5:0 16		4:5:1 17		3:5:2 18		2:5:3 19		1:5:4 20		0:5:5 21
6:4:0 22		5:4:1 23		4:4:2 24		3:4:3 25		2:4:4 26		1:4:5 27		0:4:6 28

7:3:0 29 | 6:3:1 30 | 5:3:2 31 | 4:3:3 32 | 3:3:4 33 | 2:3:5 34 | 1:3:6 35 | 0:3:7 36

8:2:0 37 | 7:2:1 38 | 6:2:2 39 | 5:2:3 40 | 4:2:4 41 | 3:2:5 42 | 2:2:6 43 | 1:2:7 44 | 0:2:8 45

9:1:0 46 | 8:1:1 47 | 7:1:2 48 | 6:1:3 49 | 5:1:4 50 | 4:1:5 51 | 3:1:6 52 | 2:1:7 53 | 1:1:8 54 | 0:1:9 55

10:0:0 56 | 9:0:1 57 | 8:0:2 58 | 7:0:3 59 | 6:0:4 60 | 5:0:5 61 | 4:0:6 62 | 3:0:7 63 | 2:0:8 64 | 1:0:9 65 | 0:0:10 66

To make a colour triangle at 2% depth of shade

The first figure in each square represents the proportion of blue, the second, yellow, and the third, red.

Make sure that the fibre is well scoured and presoaked in warm water for at least 20 minutes before dyeing. I have also learnt the hard way that some yarns still contain spinning oils, so I submit my woollen yarns to an ammonia bath as part of the scouring process. You may prefer to add the leveller or liquid detergent to the soaking water, and omit it from the dye baths.

You will need small volumes of 0.1% and 0.01% dye solutions. Levelling agents and other additives may also be reduced into solutions in the manner described in Chapter Three. Refer also to the notes on dyeing several small samples at once on p.156.

Each dye square will contain 1 gm of yarn, and the strength of the dye will be 1% solution. Using our formula from p.57:

$$\frac{W \text{ (weight of fibre) x D (depth of shade)}}{S \text{ (strength of dye)}} = V \text{ (volume of dye solution)}$$

$$\frac{1 \times 2}{1} = 2$$

Therefore the total amount of 1% dye solution for each square will be 2 ml.

Each one tenth part will 0.2 ml of 1% solution. This is too small a volume of dye solution to measure so reduce the dye strength from 1% to 0.1% strength and try again.

$$\frac{1 \times 2}{0.1} = 20 \text{ ml of 0.1% dye solution}$$

Each one tenth part is now 2 ml which is easy to measure. Refer to the diagram:

Square 1 = 0.10.0.

        0 parts blue
        10 parts yellow = 10 x 2 ml of 0.1% solution   Total 20 ml
        0 parts red

Square 42 = 3.2.5

        3 parts blue =   6 ml of 0.1% solution
        2 parts yellow =   4 ml of 0.1% solution   Total 20 ml
        5 parts red =   10 ml of 0.1% solution

Square 57 = 9.0.1

        9 parts blue =   18 ml of 0.1% solution
        0 parts yellow   Total 20 ml
        1 part red =   2 ml of 0.1% solution

Graduated triangles may be produced using dyes at any depth of shade (though all three should be the same depth of shade). A triangle at 2% depth of shade looks amazingly different from one at $1/8$% depth of shade.

To make the same triangle at $1/8$% (0.125%) depth of shade and 0.01% dye:

$$\frac{1 \times 0.125}{0.01} = 12.5 \text{ ml of 0.01% dye sloution}$$

One tenth part = 1.25 ml of 0.01% or 12.5 ml of 0.001% strength dye.

Triangles do not have to be produced purely from primary hues. Any three dyes may be used. For really subtle shades try red/brown, grey or khaki as one of the three colours.

Keeping sample records is obviously sensible. My experience has shown that records kept in some form of book, folder or chart, do not become 'lost'. My

When dyeing small test samples you need to find a method of mixing several dyes at once, otherwise dyeing seems to go on for ever.

One good method is to use a number of chemical beakers with an electric frypan as the heat source. They are initially expensive, but they are very useful for preparing colour samples or for dyeing small quantities of fibre.

An alternative is to use preserving jars in a water bath. Make sure that the water does not spill over into the dye pots. Empty tins are good, but the acid eats into the seams and they are only used once.

A 1% graduated colour triangle using the three hues Blue 3G, Yellow 4G and Red 6G. Each has a leaning towards yellow, so producing warm, earthy colours The same triangle at ¹/₈% depth of dye includes shades of peach, warm pinks, cream and smoky lavenders.

A 12 hue colour wheel dyed at a 4% depth of dye. The yellow is extremely dominant because of its high intensity, while the violet recedes because of its comparative low intensity (see p.162).

Similarly based colours are harmonious together as these colour swatches show.

Top: The primary hues all have a leaning towards yellow (G) and produce warm earthy shades.
Right: All colours are slightly 'greyed' with a complementary when mixing the dyes.
Bottom: A combination of Red B and Blue R minimizes the yellow and produces clear violets, blue-pinks and 'cooler' colours.

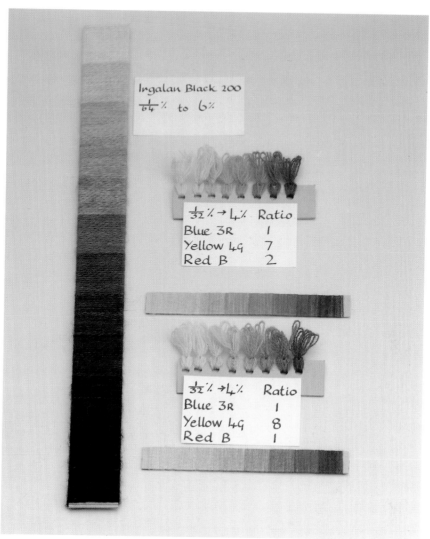

Ingalan Black 200
$\frac{1}{64}$ % to 6%

$\frac{1}{32}$% → 4% Ratio
Blue 3R ... 1
Yellow 4G ... 7
Red B ... 2

$\frac{1}{32}$% → 4% Ratio
Blue 3R ... 1
Yellow 4G ... 8
Red B ... 1

A black, grey and white value scale. The smaller samples show that one square taken from a three hue graduated triangle can be produced in a range of dye depths to give a value scale. The ratio of the three hues (Blue 3R, Yellow 4G and Red B) remains constant in each group. Only the amount of dye changes.

Blue 3R
Orange
{ 7 parts Yellow 4G
{ 3 parts Red 6G

A two colour value change square. The orange increases in value horizontally while the blue increases vertically. The complementary hues chosen produce some interesting greys.

preference is for charts with wound samples and full documentation. Whenever I have insufficient time to mount samples, I simply thread them through holes in a piece of cardboard which I label with the dye name, the colour, and the depth of shade.

Many of you will feel that colour triangle samples are inappropriate because you usually apply dye directly to the fabric or fibre. To you I recommend colour mixing trials on samples, applying the dye and fixing the dye in the usual manner. Keep them as reference material, noting which dyes were used. Note also, the difference in colour between wet and dry dyes.

COMPLEMENTARY COLOURS

Complementary colours lie diametrically opposite each other on the colour wheel. Refer back to p.151.

> Yellow complements violet (blue + red).
> Blue complements orange (yellow + red).
> Red complements green (yellow + blue).

As you can see, complementary colours together contain all of the primary colours. When complementary colours are mixed together they produce black or neutral grey.

Complementary colours are used when colour mixing to 'grey' or dull a hue. When mixing dyes using all primaries, we found that yellow and violet in proportion produced olive. Yellow/orange 'greyed' with blue/violet becomes ochre, orange with blue becomes brown, red/orange with blue/green becomes red/brown, and red with green becomes maroon. My wine/maroon bedcover is composed of a scarlet weft and a dark bottle green warp. Although dulled, the colour has more life than a plain maroon dyed cover.

BLACKS, GREYS AND BROWNS

I use a black dye to dye yarn black. I have found that when using black to 'grey' a colour, it flattens or deadens it. I prefer to use a complementary to darken a colour. The resulting maroons, navys, plums, olives, rusts, and so on, are far richer.

Greys themselves are rarely neutral grey. They may either have a leaning towards yellow, blue or red. Do not presume that because you have a collection of greys, they will look good together. Spinners of natural grey fleece should be aware of this. One 'grey' handspun and handknitted jersey makes my complexion look quite sallow, whilst another suits me much better. Greys leaning towards yellow, look better with 'warm' colours. Those towards blue look better with 'cool' colours. A grey fleece overdyed looks splendid because it naturally 'greys' the applied colours.

You may have noticed that brown does not appear within the colour wheel. There are many brown shades, but all are 'greyed' oranges, orange/yellows, or orange/reds, and their complementaries will therefore be in the blue area of the colour wheel.

So far we have been talking about colours, whether primary, secondary or complementary. However, colour has properties other than the hue or shade.

INTENSITY

Intensity refers to the brightness or dullness of a colour. Colours that are bright are intense and dull colours are less intense. Dyes are made duller and less intense by mixing them with their complementary colour.

> Red becomes brick red, which is less intense.
> Yellow becomes yellow olive, which is less intense.

The closer a colour is to a primary, the more intense it is. Yellow is of high intensity. Tone it down by using less dye, or use it sparingly if a composition of balance is required. Violet is of low intensity. You may need to use more dye, or increase the visible area of dye to achieve a composition of balanced weight of unified colours.

Look at the colour wheel produced from 4% dyes (p.158). The yellow stands out because it is so intense, and the violet recedes and looks less intense. Had I wanted a visually balanced, and more harmonious colour wheel, I could have either reduced the depth of shade of the yellow dye, or reduced the area of the yellow to a narrow strip, and at the same time increased the depth of shade or the surface area of the violet dye.

VALUE

Value means the lightness or darkness compared to a white and black scale. Look at a newspaper photograph and see how many graduations of grey there are. A painter mixes white with a colour to produce a tint, which is lighter. It becomes a higher value. He mixes black with a colour to produce a tone, which is darker. It becomes a lower value.

A dyer uses more or less dye to change the value. We refer to a greater (more dye) or lesser (less dye) **depth of shade**. If you look at a black and white photograph of skeins of yarn dyed different colours, all those appearing the same grey in the photograph will be the same value. I was astonished to see a black and white photograph of a handwoven rug with a bold distinctive design in red and green. The rug appeared an all over grey completely without design, because the colours were of equal value.

White is the lightest, the highest value. Yellow is naturally the closest hue to white, and is of high value. Black is the darkest, the lowest value, and hues close to black, such as purple and violet, have a low value.

Value cards

A very useful exercise is to make a value, or depth of shade card for reference. A black/grey/white one is probably the most useful (see illustration, p.159), but a selection of one per dye colour is an excellent method of finding out what a hue looks like in several values, for example pink to dark red. Using the calculation chart for 1 gm of fibre on p.57, dye 1 gm of fibre to depths of shade varying from

$^1/16$ % to 6 %. (Wool yarn is perhaps the most useful.) Try eight different dyes and wind them onto a piece of card to use as reference material. As before, make sure your yarn is well scoured before beginning.

Two-colour value change square for colour matching and recording

I find these colour squares really exciting to make. Only two dyes are used to complete the square of 36 dyes, and all of the shades within the square combine well together because all are related to each other. One colour (A) increases in depth of shade from $^1/16$% to 2% **horizontally**, whilst the other colour (B) increases in the same proportions **vertically**. (See illustration, p.160.) Dye for each square is mixed separately in the graduated proportions shown. Colour A is shown in the white half of each square; Colour B is shown in the shaded half.

Before you start dyeing, prepare a solution of the necessary additives and 300 ml volume of 0.1% dye solution and 300 ml volume of 0.01% solution for each of the two dyes that you have chosen. Note that the heavy lines on the chart indicate the change from the weaker 0.01% solution to the stronger 0.1% dye solution.

It is easy to calculate the amounts of dye if each dye square is produced from 1 gm of yarn. As you can see from the chart on p.57, for dyeing 1 gm of yarn you will need for:

$^1/16$%: 6.25 ml of 0.01% dye solution $^1/2$%: 5 ml of 0.1% dye solution
$^1/8$%: 12.5 ml of 0.01% dye solution   1%: 10 ml of 0.1% dye solution
$^1/4$%: 25 ml of 0.01% dye solution   2%: 20 ml of 0.1% dye solution

	Colour A in 0.01% solution			Colour A in 0.1% solution			
A	1/16%	1/8%	1/4%	1/2%	1%	2%	
B	1/16%	1/16%	1/16%	1/16%	1/16%	1/16%	Colour B in 0.01% solution
A	1/16%	1/8%	1/4%	1/2%	1%	2%	
B	1/8%	1/8%	1/8%	1/8%	1/8%	1/8%	
A	1/16%	1/8%	1/4%	1/2%	1%	2%	
B	1/4%	1/4%	1/4%	1/4%	1/4%	1/4%	
A	1/16%	1/8%	1/4%	1/2%	1%	2%	
B	1/2%	1/2%	1/2%	1/2%	1/2%	1/2%	Colour B in 0.1% solution
A	1/16%	1/8%	1/4%	1/2%	1%	2%	
B	1%	1%	1%	1%	1%	1%	
A	1/16%	1/8%	1/4%	1/2%	1%	2%	
B	2%	2%	2%	2%	2%	2%	

If you cannot remember if you have changed to the stronger dye solution, or whether you have added the second dye to the bath, throw it away and measure that dye again.

Number each square from 1–36 for identification and label the dye pots and the dyed yarn with this number. You can then refer to the square to find out that square 28, for example, was produced from Colour A at $1/2\%$ depth of shade, and Colour B at 1% depth of shade. Whatever the weight of fibre you subsequently dye to this shade, you can work out the amount of dye needed.

To mount the final 36 dyes, use double sided sticky tape to wind the yarn onto strips of card. I find it useful to attach tufts of yarn around the edge of the square. They can be removed and replaced for colour matching purposes.

A value change card can also be made by keeping one colour constant, with a second changing in percentage.

Three-colour value change triangle

Refer back to the colour change triangle you made earlier. In the same way as you have made a square with two colours, any dye square of the three-colour triangle may be used to produce a value scale of depth of shade. I have found this exercise most useful when trying to find which brown or orange produces which shade of 'cream' or 'natural'. For example, using from $1/32\%$ to 6% of dye with a mixture of 8 parts Yellow 4G, and 1 part Blue 2R, and 1 part Red B, will give a colour range from pale cream to rich brown. In all cases above, more dye has been used to produce a colour of lower value (darker).

If we mix red + yellow, each at 2%, we produce a 4% orange dye. If we mix red + violet, each at 2%, we produce a 4% red/violet. When placed beside a black and white value scale, the orange will have a higher value than the red/violet which will appear darker. A hue will have a lower value when mixed with a low value hue.

CHOOSING COLOUR COMBINATIONS

At this stage we have covered a small amount of colour theory and we have found that the finest tutor is our own experimentation. We will look at colour schemes in the same manner, beginning with some safe combinations with which to start.

Ranges of value

Choose a colour and change the value, using more or less dye to produce a range of shades. They belong to the same colour family and are therefore related. They could range from pink ($1/8\%$ depth of shade) to medium red (2% depth of shade) to strong red (4–6% depth of shade). Colour combinations such as cream, honey, gold to rich browns, or peach, coral, to maroon can be achieved with dye ranging from $1/16\%$ to 6% depth of shade. These combinations are most harmonious, very safe and comfortable. You may need to add some excitement by using the extreme ranges of light and dark to form a contrast.

Two colour value changes

All 36 individual shades produced from two dyes in a two-colour value change chart, like the one we have just prepared, are related to each other because each contains part of both dyes. Only the value of each dye has been changed. Any combination of shades from this chart is harmonious. The extremes of value or of hue can be used to form a contrast.

Change of value of two hues adjacent on the colour wheel.
Hues close to each other on the colour wheel share a relationship which can be extended by changing the value or depth of shade of each hue. For example: yellow to cream + orange to peach, or blue to ice blue + violet to lavender will be harmonious colour combinations.

Ranges of intensity
Choose a hue and gradually dull it with a complementary, or near complementary. Pure red becomes maroon and then burgundy. This could also be a progression from the outside to the inside of a colour triangle.

Goethe's Intensity Scale
We noticed that yellow was too intense within the colour wheel when all of the segments were dyed at the same depth of dye, and suggested that we either used less dye to reduce the value or we covered a smaller area with the yellow to maintain a feeling of balance. The violet could also be increased either in area or depth of dye to achieve the same effect. Goethe compared pure colours to a medium value neutral grey background and gave them simple numbers to indicate their intensity.

yellow = 9, orange = 8, red = 6, violet = 3, blue = 4, green = 6

On this scale yellow is three times stronger than violet and therefore to maintain balance only one third of the area of yellow will be used to that of violet. Red and green have the same light value and therefore may be placed in equal amounts. From this we can work out that to maintain harmony, colours of the same intensity should be used in these proportions of area:

yellow 3 orange 4 red 6 violet 9 blue 8 green 6

Here is a composition of yellow, orange and blue which is harmonious, according to Goethe's value scale.

YELLOW	ORANGE	BLUE

Analogous schemes
We can move to something a little more exciting by moving around the colour wheel. Red is a stimulating hue but if supported by Red G, Red B, red/orange and a hint of red/ violet, all of the same value, the difference is immense. It is most subtle. You may need to look closely to separate the individual colours, but the overall effect has more life.

An analogous scheme takes one segment of the colour wheel, containing colours adjacent to each other and containing one primary colour within each

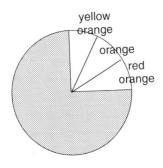

segment. An analogous scheme cannot fail because each colour is related to its neighbour by common makeup. If you are unsure of colour, start with this scheme.

If you have a colour wheel, cover it with a piece of cardboard or paper from which approximately one quarter has been removed, so that you can view the colours beneath. The scheme relies upon the colours being of equal value and intensity so:
• Keep pale colours together. Keep dark colours together.
• Keep bright colours together. Keep dull colours together.

A change of value or intensity may be reserved to form a smaller highlight or contrast within the scheme. For example: yellow/orange + yellow + yellow/green, may include a highlight of a paler or duller version of the same colours – olive, cream, peach, or pale apple used sparingly.

An analogous scheme may be extended around the wheel quite safely providing that the proportion of colour introduced reduces as you move away from the central colour.

RED/ORANGE

RED   ORANGE

less than 50%   less than 50%

RED/VIOLET   YELLOW/ORANGE

Touch of VIOLET   Touch of YELLOW

Harmony and Balance

In his book *The Elements Of Color*, Johannes Itten suggests that harmony is related to an orderly placement of colour based upon the 12-part colour wheel, with pure colours of equal value. When mixed together they produce grey. The colour groupings form triangles, squares or rectangles within the wheel. Here are some for you to try.

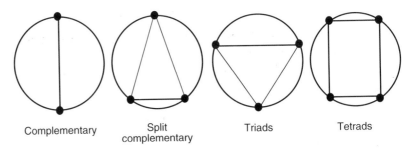

Complementary   Split complementary   Triads   Tetrads

• **Complementary pairs** are diametrically opposite.
• **Split complementary:** A hue + the colour each side of the complementary.
• **Triads:** Three colours equidistant from each other forming an equilateral triangle. For example: yellow + red + blue *or* orange + violet + green.
• **Tretrads:** Two pairs of complementaries which join to form a rectangle. For example: yellow + violet + red/orange + blue/green.

I find these combinations very pleasing, but you have to decide whether they are suitable for your project. They may not portray the impression that you wish to create. Harmony is an individual assessment by the viewer and not necessarily the wish of the creator. The proportion of each colour also needs to be taken into consideration. (See Goethe's intensity scale.)

After Image
This is a state in which the eye and the brain endeavours to restore balance or harmony. I am sure that you will have had the experience of looking at a brightly coloured object and upon closing your eyes you have been able to 'see' it again – but in a complementary colour. Try looking at a red object for some time, then look at a white or neutral grey wall. You will see the same shape reproduced in green. The eye and brain have become tired of the red light and, trying to restore balance, imagines the blue + yellow instead.

Colours are changed by their surroundings in a similar manner. A medium grey square surrounded by green appears tinged with red, and when surrounded with red, appears tinged with green. When colours are placed next to each other the after image of one colour affects the other.

For example, place blue and green together. Blue has an after image of orange, which when seen on the green makes it appear a yellowy green. Green has an after image of red so the blue appears more purple beside green than it does by itself.

If you place the same brown beside other colours you will find that:
Brown appears greener when beside red.
Brown appears blueish when beside orange.
Brown appears yellower when beside blue.

After images make colours dissimilar, pushing them further apart. Complementary colours are already as far apart as possible. The after images intensifies them, and this is why red looks more intense beside green than beside any other hue. If you wish to stress the brilliance of orange, place it beside blue of equal brilliance for maximum impact.

When the difference in value or intensity of each colour increases, the effect of after image is reduced. Medium orange appears less brilliant beside pale blue than it does next to medium blue.

CONTRASTS AND HIGHLIGHTS

Contrasts and highlights may be achieved by using:
• change of hue or colour
• change of value (lighter or darker)
• change of temperature (warm or cold)
• change of intensity (dull or bright)
• using a complementary colour.

Contrasts in value and intensity

Light, high value colours of white or yellow make anything placed beside them appear darker. On a white background:
• yellow is less dominant because it is similar to white in intensity;
• red appears to advance;
• blues and violets really stand out because they are extreme in value to white.

In the same manner, black and violet are of low value, and higher value colours placed beside them appear to advance. On a black background the blues and purples do not demand attention, but yellows, greens and reds stand out sharply.

Light looks lighter on dark and dark looks darker on light. The more extreme colours are on the white/grey/black value scale, the more they separate when placed together.

To obtain harmony or balance when using black or white in a close colour interaction, black looks best with violets and blues, and white looks best with pastels, cream/yellow, peach/orange, pastel/leaf green. The extremes in value are reduced to a minimum. To achieve a more violent or exciting reaction, these extremes may be extended.

Bright light is also intense and of high value, and colours appear more yellow in daylight, and more violet in dull light.

Complementary colours for contrast

A colour appears most intense next to its complementary. Think how many colour advertisements show something bright orange surrounded by an equally bright blue. Blue appears more blue next to orange, and orange more orange next to blue.

Small areas of complementary colour cause visual contrast, which can be most interesting. They are used to add excitement, to interest the eye and to relieve an ultra harmonious situation. However, when blended together in equal or near equal proportions, either visually or literally – by knitting, weaving or spinning – the result is as if the pigments had been mixed together. They become greyed or dulled.

Return to the blue vase. It reflects the blue colour wave lengths. If you mix blue yarn and orange yarn, the eye sees the reflected blue light waves and the red and yellow light waves (orange), and mixes them together to make browns or greys.

I have met people who have been too timid to use a complementary as a highlight. Please try it. The amount used is very small, but adds to the visual excitement. A 'too comfortable' combination is lifted to an 'interesting' stage. Used in equal proportions it will dull its complementary, but used as a spot or flash of colour in spinning, or in a small amount placed in juxtaposition to its complementary in a design, it will be most effective.

Opposing sides of the colour wheel give a feeling of either warmth or cool, and therefore the complementary also introduces an apparent temperature change, often providing relief. When introducing yellow to a violet scheme, the proportion of yellow will need to be reduced to retain harmony, because of the extreme difference in intensity.

OTHER CONSIDERATIONS

Viewing distance

Dyers are mainly concerned with textiles. Before choosing colour combinations a few practical considerations need to be taken into account. One important factor is from what distance your textile is to be viewed. Is it seen flat on a floor or wall? Is it viewed when folded or draped? Is it a tablecloth which is designed to allow cutlery and dinnerware to be supported visually, or is it a small highlight area such as a cushion, which gives added colour and is a complete design within itself?

Rugs and wall pieces may convey a meaning, a feeling or a statement. The colours will be chosen with that intention. They will be mainly placed in juxtaposition so that they respond to each other and to their background, and will be seen in entirety.

When viewing fabrics from the natural position of wearer to viewer, small spots of colour are visually mixed and the results will be similar to those when mixing pigments and dyes. Fabrics containing several colours not too distant apart on the colour wheel catch the light when viewed from different angles, or when folded or draped, and become interesting to the viewer. However, the viewing distance of a fabric cannot be dictated, therefore it must look good from close and distant proximity.

Fabric artists have less of a problem with viewing distance than spinners and weavers, because fabric artists usually work with larger areas of colour.

Spinners and weavers are literally twisting colours together and must remember that equal amounts of complementary colours produce a dull sometimes muddy overall colour. Dull colours subdue their partners, and extremes of intensity or value appear spotty and unrelated in small areas such as in handspun yarn, although some form of highlight adds tremendous interest.

When you have doubts about colour choices, reproduce your idea in paint, yarn or fibre, and view from the usual distance.

Emotional response

Once you understand why certain colours appear comfortable or exciting together and why others are discordant, all 'rules' can be broken. An artist uses colour freely to express feeling or uses them for their symbolic meaning. Make a personal individual response to colour without the limitations of colour 'theories' and see what develops. Then make the judgement 'has it worked?'.

Some people have an inbuilt feeling for colour and many use interesting colour combinations that do not fit into any standard colour grouping. I personally shun any books that state 'these colours sit well together'. The decision or choice of colour is so detached from me that it does not become part of my created work. Choosing colour either instinctively or by calculated combinations is part of the creativity of a piece.

Each person has an individual reaction to colour, which may or may not depend upon the emotional or psychological feeling each has at the time of viewing. There are days when I delight in using pure colour, and days when I am more comfortable with dull shades. I dislike working with brown and usually avoid doing so, but when I need to, I make the situation more comfortable by choosing logical highlights.

Colours convey certain symbolic meaning. Yellow suggests sunlight, warmth, life-giving forces, and promotes sociability and mental stimulation. Red suggests fire, passion, festivity, and is used in posters for its dominant features. Green is natural and restful. Blue/green slows down the breathing rate, promoting calm. Blue is cool and calm, suggesting water and clear summer skies, whilst violet is spiritual and mysterious.

Sources of inspiration and areas of study

If we are not visually aware of our surroundings we will not be able to use colour successfully. We are surrounded by natural colour and yet many of us do not really see it. Rock faces, tree barks, autumn leaves, sunrise or sunset skies have provided starting places for many successful creations. Take a photograph, take a sample, or write what you see in a notation that a dyer might understand. For example: Red B + Blue R, with a touch of yellow, maroon and rust and a hint of lime green, (Blue G + yellow).

Magazines contain reproductions of colour photographs designed to convey the impression of a place or product. If you find a picture with colours that you really like, analyse the colours into complementary colours, greyed colours , bright or dull shades, and work out the proportions of each that complete the composition. Ask what feeling the picture intends to convey and whether it is suitable for your work.

Recently I have been interested in watching pop record videos on my television screen. Although basically advertising material, many are art forms in themselves and use colour to evoke mood or atmosphere. If you do not enjoy the music you can turn the sound level down!

Studying the manner in which artists use colour is both profitable and pleasurable. I am a frequent visitor to art galleries, exhibitions and to the public library. I have been particularly excited by the works of Monet, Pissarro, and Renoir, by Matisse, Cezanne, Bonnard and by Klee. I am sure that you will also have your favourites.

In conclusion, following theories rigidly inhibits an artist's spontaneous use of colour. If you work instinctively without any preconceived ideas, you are more likely to use colours for the impression that they create or for their symbolic meaning. If your colour combinations fail to portray your intention, or are discordant when you intended harmony, reference to colour theory will certainly be helpful. Acknowledge your mistakes because they are part of the learning process.

Understanding colour theories alone will not bring you expertise or lead to confidence in the use of colour, but with a basic knowledge and plenty of experimentation, you will be pointing in the right direction.

Mordants
Alum – aluminium sulphate
Chrome – potassium dichromate or sodium dichromate
Iron – ferrous sulphate
Tin – stannous chloride
Copper – copper sulphate

Assistants

Acetic acid enables dye to bond to protein fibres

Ammonium sulphate releases acid during dyeing of protein fibres

Calcium hydroxide slaked lime: an alkali for indigo dyeing

Gutta: colourless rubber latex resist

Methylated spirit: denatured alcohol

Resist salts prevent dye from decomposing during dyeing. Resist salt L, Matexil PAL, Sitol, Ludigol, Nacon, Revatol are trade names associated with particular dyes

Sodium alginate used as a thickener for dyes: Manutex, Keltex (also in Polycell paste)

Sodium bicarbonate, baking soda: alkali used when painting dyes on cellulose fibres

Sodium bichromate, hydrogen peroxide: an oxidizing agent

Sodium carbonate, washing soda or soda ash: an alkali.

Sodium chloride: common salt

Sodium dithionite, formerly sodium hydrosulphite: used for indigo vat dyeing – an alkali

Sodium hexame taphosphate – water softener

Sodium hydroxide, caustic soda: an alkali for naphthol dyeing

Sodium hydrosulphite (now sodium dithionite): used for indigo vat dyeing – an alkali

Sodium hypochlorite: a bleach (Scrubbs ammonia is 9%, N.Z. Cloudy 6%)

Sodium sulphate, Glauber's salt: slows down ability of the dye to bond with the fibre – a leveller

Tannic acid: preparation for cotton dyeing 'galling'

Wetting agents, levellers: Albegal A and B, SETT, Lissapol, Rewin W, Sandozin AMP, Wetter, and others

MEASURES
Measures given are rounded to the nearest '5'. Remember to use either metric or imperial measures in a recipe, since they may not be exactly equivalent.

Ounces to grams

1 oz = 30 gm	7 oz = 200 gm
2 oz = 55 gm	8 oz = 225 gm
3 oz = 85 gm	10 oz = 285 gm
4 oz = 115 gm	12 oz = 340 gm
5 oz = 140 gm	14 oz = 400 gm
6 oz = 170 gm	16 oz (1 lb) = 455 gm

Fluid measures
1 fluid ounce = 28 ml
8 fluid ounces = 225 ml
16 fluid ounces = 455 ml
1 gallon = approx. 4.5 litres
$1/2$ gallon = approx. 2 litres
1 quart = approx. 1 litre
1 pint = approx. 600 ml

1 fluid ounce weighs 1 ounce. There are 20 fluid ounces in a pint and roughly 40 to 1 quart (1 litre).

Spoon measures
Metric $1/4$ teaspoon (tsp) = 1.25 ml
Metric $1/2$ tsp = 2.5 ml
Metric tsp = 5 ml
Metric dessertspoon (dsp) = 10 ml
Metric tablespoon (tbsp) = 15 ml

Dry and liquid measures are given in millilitres. 1 ml of water weighs 1 gm therefore 1 tsp also holds 5 gm.

Cup measures
1 metric cup = 250 ml
4 metric cups = 1 litre (1000 ml)
Half a litre jug = 2 cups (500 ml)

BIBLIOGRAPHY

Natural Dyeing

Bolton, Eileen M., *Lichens For Vegetable Dyeing*, Studio Books, London, 1960.

Botanic Garden Record, *Shuttle, Spindle and Dyepot*, 1968–75.

Bliss, Anne, 'Linen Dyes', *Handwoven*, March–April 1989, Interweave Press, USA.

Brooklyn Botanic Garden Record, Natural Plant Dyeing, Vol 29, No. 2. New York.

Davidson, Mary Frances, *The Dye Pot*, Gatlinburg, Tenn. USA, 1950.

Dyer, Anne, *Dyes From Natural Sources*, G. Bell and Sons, London, 1976.

Gerber, Frederick H., *Indigo and the Antiquity of Dyeing*, Frederick H. Gerber, 1977.

Gerber, Frederick H., *Cochineal and the Insect Dyes*, Frederick H. Gerber, 1978.

Gerber, Frederick H., 'The Investigative Method of Natural Dyeing', Reprints from *Handweaver and Craftsman*, Brooklyn.

Goodwin, Jill, *A Dyer's Manual*, Pelham Books, London, 1982.

Handweavers and Spinners Guild of Victoria, The, *Dyemaking with Australian Flora*, Rigby Limited, Sydney, Australia, 1974.

Lloyd Joyce, *Dyes From Plants*, Joyce Lloyd, Wellington, New Zealand, 1971.

Mairet, Ethel, *Vegetable Dyes*, Faber, London, 1st ed. 1916, 10th printing, London 1948.

Martin, William and Child, John, *New Zealand Lichens*, A.H. and A.W. Reed, Wellington, NZ, 1972.

Milner, Ann, *Natural Wool Dyes And Recipes*, John McIndoe, Dunedin, New Zealand, 1971.

Morris Lorna, 'Solar Dyeing', *The Web*, November 1981, New Zealand.

Orchiston, Rene, '*Sticta coronata*', *The Web*, March 1972, New Zealand.

Simpson, L.E and Wier, M., *The Weaver's Craft*, Dryad Press, Leicester, England, 1967.

Thompson, Francis, *Harris Tweed*, David and Charles, Newton Abbot, 1969.

Thurston, Violetta, *The Use of Vegetable Dyes*, Dryad Press, Leicester, England, 1967.

Weigle, Palmy, *Ancient Dyes For Modern Weavers*, Watson-Guptill, New York, 1974.

Wickens, Hetty, *Natural Dyes For Spinners And Weavers*, Batsford, London.

Dyeing

Australian Forum for Textile Arts, The, *Dyeing For Fibres And Fabrics*, Kangaroo Press, 1987.

Dawson, Pam, *How to Paint on Silk*, Search Press, Great Britain, 1988.

Dyrenforth, Noel, *The Technique of Batik*, Batsford, London, 1988.

Gilmour, Pat, *Dyes And Dyeing*, Society for Education Through Art, London, 1966.

Knutson, Linda, *Synthetic Dyes For Natural Fibres*, Interweave Press, 1986.

Maile, Anne, *Tie and Dye Made Easy*, Mills and Boon, London, Taplinger Publishing Company, New York, 1971.

Proctor, Richard M. and Lew, Jennifer F., *Surface Design For Fabric*, University of Washington Press, 1984.

Robinson, Stuart and Patricia, *Exploring Fabric Printing*, Mills and Boon, London, Charles T. Branford Company, Massachusetts, 1972.

Simmons, Max, *Dyes and Dyeing*, Thomas Nelson, Australia, 1983.

Tomita, J. and N., *Japanese Ikat Weaving: The Techniques of Kasuri*, Routledge and Kegan Paul, 1982.

Tompson, Frances and Tony, *Synthetic Dyeing for Spinners, Weavers, Knitters and Embroiderers*, David and Charles, 1987.

Van Gelder, Lydia, *Ikat*, Watson-Guptill Publications, New York, 1980.

Colour

Birren, Faber, *The Textile Colorist*, Van Nostrand Reinhold Company, New York, 1980.

Cheatham, Frank R., Cheatham Jane Hart, Haler Sheryl A., *Design Concepts And Applications*, Prentice-Hall, Inc., Englewood Cliffs, N.J., 1983.

Duncan, Molly, and Bull, George, *Exploring Colour And Design*, A.H. and A.W. Reed Ltd, Wellington, New Zealand, 1978.

Grumbacher, *Color Compass*, M. Grumbacher, Inc., New York 1972.

Itten, Johannes, *The Elements Of Color*, Van Nostrand Reinhold Company, New York, 1970.

Klein, Bernat, *Eye for Colour*, Bernat Klein, Scotland with Collins, London, 1965.

Tidball, Harriet, *Color and Dyeing*, Shuttle Craft Guild, California, USA, 1965.

Weigle, Palmy, *Color Exercises For The Weaver*, Watson-Guptill, New York, 1976.

Fibres and Other

Austin, Bridget, *The Feltmaker's Handbook*, Pitman, 1988.

Field, Anne, *The Ashford Book Of Spinning*, Benton Ross, Auckland, New Zealand, 1986.

Fletcher, Joan, *Silk In New Zealand*, NZ Spinning, Weaving and Woolcrafts Society Inc., 1986.

Milner, Ann, *I Can Spin A Different Thread*, John McIndoe, Dunedin, New Zealand, 1979.

Sparks, Kathy, Wipplinger, Michele, 'Dyeing Angora Rabbit', Craft Dyers' Guild, Issue No. 29, June 1989.

ASHFORD DISTRIBUTORS

New Zealand
Ashford Handicrafts Ltd, PO Box 474, Ashburton.
Tel. (03) 308-9087, Fax (03) 308-8664

Australia
Ashford Handicrafts Ltd, Traveller's Rest, Snowy
Mountain Highway, Cooma NSW 2630.
Tel. 008-026397, 064-524422. Fax 064-524523.
Ashford weaving looms and spinning wheels are
sold throughout Australia. For the name of your
nearest dealer please contact our branch office for
details.

Austria
Alles Zum Gesunden Bauen and Wohnen, Ing Volkmar
Baurecker, Hirrshgasse 22A, 4020 Linz. Tel. (0732)
277285

Belgium
Artisans, Boulevard Paul Janson, 11-13, 6000
Charleroi. Tel. (071) 316505

Canada
Treenway Crafts Ltd, 725 Caledonia, Victoria BC, V8T
1B4. Tel. (604) 383-1661
Samson Angoras, RR1 Brantford, Ontario N3T SL4.
Tel. (519) 788 5650

Denmark
Elsa Krogh, Havndalvej 40, 9550 Mariager.
Tel. (98) 542253
Spindegrej, Fjellebrosvejen 25, 5762 V. Sterninge. Tel.
(09) 244030
Kip Garn, Hersegade 12, 4000 Roskilde. Tel. 02372349

Finland
Toijalan Kaidetehdas KY, PL 25, 37801 Toijala.
Tel. (937) 21095

Germany
Fredrich Traub KG, D-7065 Winterbach, Schorndorfer
Str Be 18. Tel (07181) 77055

Ireland
Craftspun Yarns Ltd, Johnstown-Naas, County Kildare.
Tel. (045) 76881

Japan
Ananda Co Ltd, 1221 Shimojo, Nagasaka-Cho,
kitakoma-Gun, Yamanashi. Tel. 0551 324215

Ocean Trading Co Ltd, 8th Floor, 1-2, Kyoto Toshiba
Bldg, 25 Hira-machi, Saiin, Ukyo-ku, Kyoto.
Tel. (075) 314 8720
Mariya Handicrafts Ltd, Kita-1, Nishi-3, Chuo-Ku,
Sapporo 060. Tel. (011) 221 3307
Sanyo Trading Co, Minamisenju, 5-9-6-905 Arakawa-
ku, Tokyo 116. Tel. (03) 801 9020
Ishida Noriko, 502 Daitshu Building, Imagawa 2-1-67,
Fukuoka

Korea
Haelim Trading Co Ltd, CPO Box 1653, Seoul.
Tel. 752 8271
Fine Corporation, CPO Box 6718, Seoul.
Tel. (02) 7791894

Netherlands
Falkland Natuurgarens, Bosstraat 33, 3971 XA
Driebergen. Tel. 03438-18155

Norway
Spinninger, Boks 36, 1362 Billingstad. Tel.(02) 846022

Papua New Guinea
Eastern Highland Cultural Centre, c/- Mrs Anne
Montgomery, Box 37, Kaimantu.

Sweden
Gundruns Ullbod, Ulunda 5462, 19991Enkopenj. Tel.
(0171) 39995

Switzerland
Spinnstube, Sch miedengasse 6, 2502 Biel.
Tel. (032) 22 2960
Spycher – Handwerk, 4953 Schwarzenbach, b. Huttwil.
Tel. (063) 721152.

United Kingdom
Haldane & Co, Gateside by Cupar, Fife KY14 7ST.
Tel. (03376) 469, Fax (03376) 507
Ashford weaving looms and spinning wheels are
sold throughout the UK. For the name of your
nearest dealer, please contact our UK distributor
Haldane & Co for details.

United States
Crystal Palace Yarns, 3006 San Pablo Ave, Berkeley
CA 94702. Tel. (415) 548 9988

INDEX

Acidity, levels of, 59
Acids, added after natural dyeing, 24
After image, 167
Alkalinity, levels of, 59
Alkalis
    added after natural dyeing, 24
    used with indigo, 45

Batch ageing, 102, 104
Batik, 77, 87, 108, 122, 126-28

Cold pad batch dyeing, 88, 96, 98-102
Colour, 150-70
    analogous schemes, 165
    contrasts, 167-68
    emotional response to, 169
    harmony and balance, 166
    intensity, 162, 165
    mixing for cold pad batch methods,
    96
    mixing, 151-53
    sources of inspiration for, 170
    triangles, 154-55, 157
    value, 51, 162-65, 168
    viewing distance, 169
Colours
    complementary, 161, 167, 168
    intermediate, 150
    primary, 150
    secondary, 150
Colour wheel, 50, 150, 151

Depth of shade, 51, 52, 162
Diazo salts, 91
Dip dyeing, 80, 112, 137
Dribbling dyes, 115, 116
Dye bath dyeing, 24-25, 59-74, 75-94,
139-41
    in a microwave oven, 142-44
    novelty effects with, 112-14
Dye crayons, 139
Dye labels, reading, 50
Dye powder, concentration, 51
Dye powder
    determining quantity, 51-52
    pasting, 55
Dye solutions, 56-58
Dyes, chemical, see Index of Dyes
Dyes, natural, 27-48
    substantive, 20
Dyes, unlevel, reasons for, 60

Equipment, 13-15, 49, 92, 96

Felt, dyeing wool for, 146
Felting, unwanted, 10, 11, 25, 146
Fabrics and fibres, descriptions, 9-13,
139
    Cellulose, 9-10, 13
        bleaching, 13
        chemical dye baths for, 75-94
        chemical dye types suitable for,

75-77, 106-11
        creative dyeing on, 118-28
        direct dye application methods,
        104-11
        mordanting, 21-22
        preparation for dyeing, 12-13, 58
        tannic acid bath for, 22
    Commercial yarns, preparation for
    dyeing, 11
    Nylon, 9, 67
    Protein, 9, 10-11
        chemical dye baths for, 59-74
        chemical dye types suitable for,
        61-63, 103
        direct dye application methods,
        95-103
        felting, unwanted, 10, 11, 25, 146
        mordanting, 20
        novelty dyeing of, 112-18
        preparation for dyeing, 10-13, 58
    Silk, 9, 10, 75, 77
        direct dye application methods,
        130-31
        liquid dyes for, 137-38
        marbled effects on, 131, 135
        watercolour effects on, 131, 134
        mordanting, 20
        preparation for dyeing, 11-12, 129
    Synthetic, 9, 13, 77, 139-41
        preparation for dyeing, 13
        chemical dye baths for, 139-41
        direct application methods, 140-41
Fibres, natural, for paper making, 147
Fixing methods, 104-05

Goethe's intensity scale, 165
Gutta, 130, 131

Heat transfer method, 141
Hot exhaust dyeing see Dye bath

Ikat, 125
Indican, plants bearing see Natural
    dyestuffs
Indigo see Natural dyestuffs
Injection dyeing, 116, 145

Kasuri, 123, 124, 125

Levellers, 60, 64, 78
Lichens see Natural dyestuffs
Liquor ratio, 14, 16, 60
Loog, 92

Measures, 58, 172
Microwave ovens, 142-45
Mordants, 20-24
Mordanting, 20-22, 112

Natural dyeing, 17-48
    novelty effects with, 112
    procedure, 24-25

for felt-making, 146
Natural dyestuffs, 19-20, 27-48
    berries and fruits, 19, 29
    brazilwood, 43
    cochineal, 40
    flowers, 27-28
    for paper-making, 150-51
    frozen, 19
    gum tree scale, 32
    indican, 47
    indigo, 44-48, 89, 122
    leaves, 19, 31-32
    lichens, 19, 33-39
    logwood, 42
    madder, 41
    onion skins, 19, 32
    poisonous, 19-20
    roots, 30
    storage, 19
    tree barks, 19, 30-31
Novelty dyeing, 112-28
    in a microwave oven, 144-45

Orchil acids, 33-34

Padding, mixtures, 88, 95, 96, 101
Painting dyes, 115, 117, 118
Paper, handmade, dyeing, 147-49
Percentage dyeing, 51, 55-58
Percentage stock solutions, 56-58
Print pastes, 107, 108, 110, 140, 141

Random effects, 111, 140
Record-keeping, 18, 19, 156
Resist dyeing, 119-28, 130, 131
Resist salts, 104

Safety, 13, 56, 60
Salt, addition to natural dyes, 24, 40
Screen printing, 95, 107, 109, 118
Shibori, 119, 124
Solar dyeing, 26
Space dyeing, 112
Spraying dyes, 115, 116, 118
Stock paste, 95, 104, 107
Stock solutions, percentage, 56-58
Substantive dyes, 20
Suffix meanings, 50, 51

Tannic acid bath, 21-22
Tie dyeing, 80, 87, 113, 144
Tjanting, 126, 127
Tritik, 119

Unlevel dyes, reasons for, 60

Value change scales, 157, 159, 160,
    156, 162-64

Warp painting, 117
Water softener, 75, 104
Wetting agents, 60

INDEX OF CHEMICAL DYES

Names in **bold** type are dye classes; the remainder are dye brand names.

12164